The Landing Beaches

Jean QUELLIEN
PROFESSOR OF CONTEMPORARY HISTORY AT THE UNIVERSITY OF CAEN
AND SECOND WORLD WAR specialist

A PROLIFIC AUTHOR,
HIS MOST FAMOUS PUBLICATIONS WITH THE MÉMORIAL DE CAEN PUBLISHING ARE :
• *NORMANDY 44* • *D-DAY AND BATTLE OF NORMANDY* • *THE RESISTANCE*

Translation by John RITCHIE

Le Mémorial de Caen

ÉDITIONS MÉMORIAL DE CAEN - ESPL. EISENHOWER -BP 6261 - 14066 CAEN CEDEX 4 - FRANCE
TÉL: +33(0)2 31 06 06 44

contents

From Dunkirk

to the Normandy Beaches

● DUNKIRK, early June 1940. An unbelievable noria of ships of every imaginable size managed to evacuate the nearly 350,000 British and French soldiers who were trapped in a narrow pocket on the North Sea coast following the lightning German offensive that had been launched three weeks previously. At that tra-

The Genesis of *OVERLORD*

HOLDING THE LINE!

• Winston Churchill was the perfect
embodiment of British tenacity •

• The raid on Dieppe •

Operation Jubilee, launched on 19th August 1942, was a gory
fiasco. Around 4,000 men (mainly Canadians) were killed,
wounded or taken prisoner.

Almost exactly four years later the British were indeed to set foot on French soil again, in Normandy, in the company of Americans and Canadians on a certain 6th June 1944. The route from Britain to Normandy turned out to be much longer than the actual distance separating them might have suggested. It was also more tortuous. Of course, the USSR's entry into the war in June 1941, then America's in December of that same year put an end to Great Britain's isolation, but it was still necessary to find agreement on strategy.

The British urged caution in the face of the impatience of the Soviets, who were clamouring for the opening of a "second front", and the Americans' desire to lose no time in attacking the Third Reich directly, in order to

• Eisenhower and Montgomery surrounded by the Overlord general staff •

1944

YEAR OF DECISION
"The supreme effort has still to be made".
Rt. Hon. W. L. Mackenzie King

• Canadian propaganda poster •

enable them to move against Japan as early as possible. The British advised attacking the Reich's periphery, with the aim weakening the adversary before delivering the fatal blow. The tragic outcome of the raid on Dieppe in August 1942, which cost the lives of over a thousand men, indisputably confirmed Churchill's contention that an amphibious assault on the coasts of occupied France would be very premature. So, like it or no, the Americans were constrained to accept the British strategy that led the Allies to land first in North Africa in November 1942, then in Sicily in July 1943 and finally in Italy two months later.

In return for these concessions, the question closest to their hearts was put back on the agenda: the great cross-Channel offensive. The principle had been agreed upon in Casablanca in 1943. During the Trident conference, which took place in May in Washington, the vast landings project that had been presented by the Americans as early as spring 1942 under the code-name "Round up" was brought back down off the shelves where the British had left it and re-baptised "Overlord".

The exact location of the assault had yet to be defined. The Quadrant conference, which took place in Quebec in August 1943, decided it should be on the Seine Bay coast rather than in the Pas-de-Calais, the latter being judged to be too predictable a choice with regard to the Germans, because of the shorter distance the assailants would be required to travel. The date settled on for the launch of the operation was the beginning of May 1944. The slowness of their progress in Italy merely reinforced the Allies' need to concentrate their efforts on the launch preparation of Overlord. The American General Eisenhower, who stepped in as Commander-in-Chief in December 1943, and his deputy, the British General Montgomery, agreed to widen the initial assault sector, which they judged to be too narrow, and to engage larger numbers of troops. This made longer preparations necessary; D-Day was postponed for a month, until the beginning of June 1944. ■

The Atlantic Wall

• The Atlantic Wall under construction •

Contrary to Hitler's hopes, the brutal offensive he launched against the USSR in June 1941 did not result in a decisive victory. The Red Army, which was at first routed, regrouped outside Moscow in December. Henceforth, the Eastern front was to swallow up a growing number of divisions, obliging the German general staff make dangerous reductions in the forces on the Western front, under the command of Marshal von Rundstedt since 1942.

Under these circumstances, the fear of an Allied invasion on the French coast, heightened by the United States' entry into the war, pushed Hitler to give the order to begin construction of an impressive defensive system, which was soon to become known as the "Atlantic Wall", in December 1941.

The work began in the spring of 1942, but was still not finished in June 1944. The scale of the task entrusted to the Todt Organisation was, admittedly, colossal, as it required the construction of around 15,000 concrete structures of varying shapes and sizes. As a consequence of the raid on Dieppe, priority was given to defence of the ports, which were transformed into veritable fortresses bristling with guns and practically impregnable by frontal assault. Long range, heavy-duty batteries, whose business it was to keep an invasion fleet at bay, were established along the coasts between them. There were thirty-odd such batteries between the fortresses in Le Havre and Cherbourg, notably at Saint-Marcouf-Crisbec, Azeville, Maisy, la Pointe-du-Hoc, Longues, Ver, Ouistreham, etc.

Marshall Rommel, who was given the mission of inspecting the Atlantic Wall at the end of 1943 and was immediately afterwards appointed commander of Army Group B charged with the coastal defences between the Loire and the North Sea, quickly detected weaknesses in the system. He gave particular attention to the Seine Bay sector, which to his mind had been neglected as the Germans had been concentrating on the Pas-de-Calais.

• Marshal Rommel on an inspection tour of the beaches •

• **German propaganda poster** •

On his instructions, concrete pillboxes with thick walls were hastily built to protect the heavy artillery, often situated in open trenches or vats, from aerial bombardment. Above all, Rommel multiplied the smaller fortifications all along the coast, the Widerstandnesten (WN) or "resistance nests" that were equipped with medium bore guns, machine-guns or mortars and whose objective was the close-range defence of the beaches against assault troops. The shores themselves were covered with all sorts of obstacles, designed to rip the

• **Part of the WN 103 near Ravenoville (Manche)** •

bottoms out of landing barges or blow them up.

However, he did not receive permission from the Wehrmacht top brass to station armoured divisions near to the coast in sufficient numbers to be able to repel the Allies back into the sea through vigorous counter-attack. He left his headquarters in La Roche-Guyon on 5th June with the intention of persuading the Führer to grant him this authorisation... a few hours before the decisive event itself. ∎

• **The 88-mm gun bunker on the sea-wall at Ver-sur-Mer** •

The Allies' Preparations

• Amphibious "DD" tanks •

• **Operation P.L.U.T.O.** • (Pipe Line Under The Ocean)

Miles of flexible pipe line were wound around this bobbin (called "Conun") and destined to be laid on the ocean floor between the Isle of Wight and the continent in order to provide fresh supplies of fuel for the Allies.

From the spring of 1943 onwards, the general staff run by General Morgan, COSSAC (Chief of Staff to the Supreme Allied Commander) got down to the business of preparing the invasion on the coast of north-western France.

As a result of their tragic experience in Dieppe, the Allies renounced launching a frontal attack on a port and chose to land directly on the beaches. However, as they needed facilities for the landing of the considerable quantities of men, vehicles and supplies required for the success of the operation, they rallied to the audacious idea launched by Winston Churchill himself. This involved building all the different parts of two artificial harbours, which would cross the Channel behind the invasion fleet in order to be assembled on site. In parallel, General Percy Hobart and his teams of engineers were working on the development of a series of special machines. Amongst them, the famous DD (Duplex Drive) amphibious tanks, designed to be launched at sea and to head for the shore under their own steam, in order to give the

artillery support to the first waves of assault that their predecessors had so cruelly lacked at Dieppe. Others were designed to clear the beaches of the different obstacles with which they were covered, opening breaches in mine-fields and enabling the troops to cross walls and anti-tank trenches quickly.

As for the special services, they were busy misleading the Germans as to the Allies' intentions; within the framework of the "Fortitude" misinformation operation they multiplied the clues hinting at an attack in the Pas-de-Calais.

With support from war bonds, the British, American and Canadian factories strove day and night to furnish the gigantic arsenal of the Allied armies with guns, tanks, lorries, landing barges etc. Finally, as part of operation "Bolero", hundreds of thousands of American soldiers

• UA tribute to operation P.L.U.T.O. :
The "Essor" monument in Port-en-Bessin •

• American propaganda poster promoting the sale
of war bonds •

arrived in England during the first months of 1944.

With spring came the massive aerial bombardment of the Atlantic Wall, radar stations, road and rail bridges, stations and air-fields. D-Day was approaching!

Its precise date depended on a whole series of parameters. First, it had to be on a full moon night in order to facilitate the task of the paratroops that were to make drops at either extremity of the landing sector. The amphibious assault itself would have to be made at dawn, at mid-rising tide in order to avoid the obstacles installed on the beaches by Rommel. The day finally settled on was 5th June, with the possibility of postponing until the next day or the day after. The tempest that blew up unexpectedly in the Channel forced Eisenhower to delay the departure when troops were already on board their ships. However, trusting in the information from the meteorological services that forecast a slight improve-

ment over the following few hours, he decided to launch the operation on 6th June. Conditions were still far from ideal, as there was, notably, a heavy swell, but a further postponement would have delayed the invasion for several weeks, and run the risk of depriving the Allies' projects of their impetus and the indispensable element of surprise. ■

• Southampton, early June. Canadian troops awaiting their
departure for France •

The Landings

• 0545 hours : the American battleship USS Arkansas opening fire •

The events on 6th June began unfolding shortly after midnight, when the British paratroops dropped between the Orne and the Dives. Then it was the Americans' turn to parachute into the Cotentin. Meanwhile, a thousand RAF heavy bombers bombarded the ten heavy artillery batteries in the Seine Bay considered to be the most dangerous. At daybreak, the 8th US Air Force took over from them, followed by the tactical aviation.

At dawn, the disbelieving Germans discovered a sea covered in thousands of ships. Lulled into a false sense of security by the bad weather - a priori unsuitable for an invasion - and blinded by the destruction of their radar systems over the preceding weeks, they had not seen the immense Allied armada as it approached. Now it was too late to react. At 0545 hours the warships opened fire on the coastal defences.

At 0630 hours the first American assault waves hit the beaches at Utah and Omaha. In the British and Canadian sectors, off Gold, Juno and Sword, the attack was launched an hour later, to compensate for the differences in tide times along the coast.

With the exception of Omaha, where the outcome of the battle hung in the balance for hours and hours, the Atlantic Wall was mercilessly rent asunder everywhere, and the Allies penetrated inland, under the protection of the air forces, omnipresent in the skies. On the beaches, the reinforcement units were coming in at a high rate.

For the time being, the Germans were unable to check the offensive. They were bogged down due to the dithering of their high command and the destruction of a part of their means of communication through sabotage by the Resistance. The only armoured division

• The first assault wave approaching Omaha Beach •

• British armour landing at Ver-sur-Mer •

• Canadian propaganda poster •

rubble, causing the death of 3,000 civilians. By the evening of 6th June, the Allies had landed over 155,000 soldiers and 20,000 vehicles. Their losses (killed, wounded and disappeared) numbered about 10,000 men, which was considerably fewer than had been predicted. With the exception of Omaha, where the Americans were still fighting with their backs to the sea, the bridgeheads had been developed six miles or so inland. Nevertheless, not all of D-Day's objectives had been achieved. Although Bayeux was liberated the next day, Caen was another matter ; the British and Canadians were not to capture it until 9th July, a whole month after the estimated date.

Whereas the invasion succeeded with relatively little fighting, the liberation of Normandy was to take much longer and be much more trying than was at first imagined. The Germans regrouped and put up fierce resistance everywhere. The Allies were to be thwarted for many long weeks both around Caen, which was protected by the formidable steel rampart of the Panzer divisions, and in the Cotentin, where the Americans were to become bogged down in the exhausting "battle of the hedgerows". It was not until the end of July that the decisive breakthrough, resulting from operation Cobra, was finally achieved to the west of Saint-Lô. One month later, the debris of the German armies that managed to escape from the Falaise pocket, where they had allowed themselves to become trapped, crossed the Seine and quit the major part of French territory without further ado. ■

LES ARMEES ALLIEES DEBARQUENT

near the coast, the 21st Panzer, which was a victim of contradictory orders, acted but to no great effect. During the evening and night of 6th to 7th June, in order to slow the arrival of enemy reinforcements, the Allied aviation systematically reduced ten Lower Normandy towns to

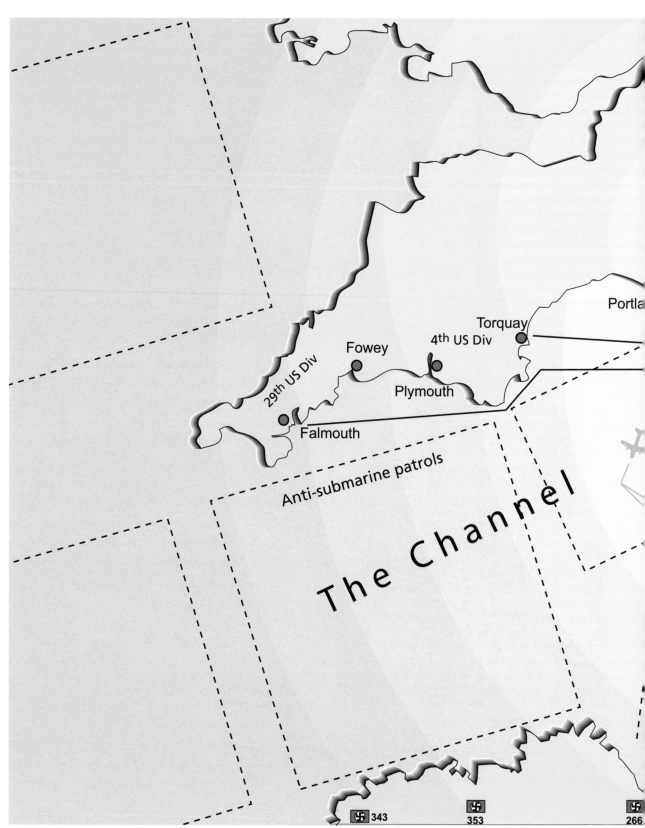

Portla

Torquay

4th US Div

Fowey

29th US Div

Plymouth

Falmouth

Anti-submarine patrols

The Channel

🏴 343

🏴 353

🏴 266

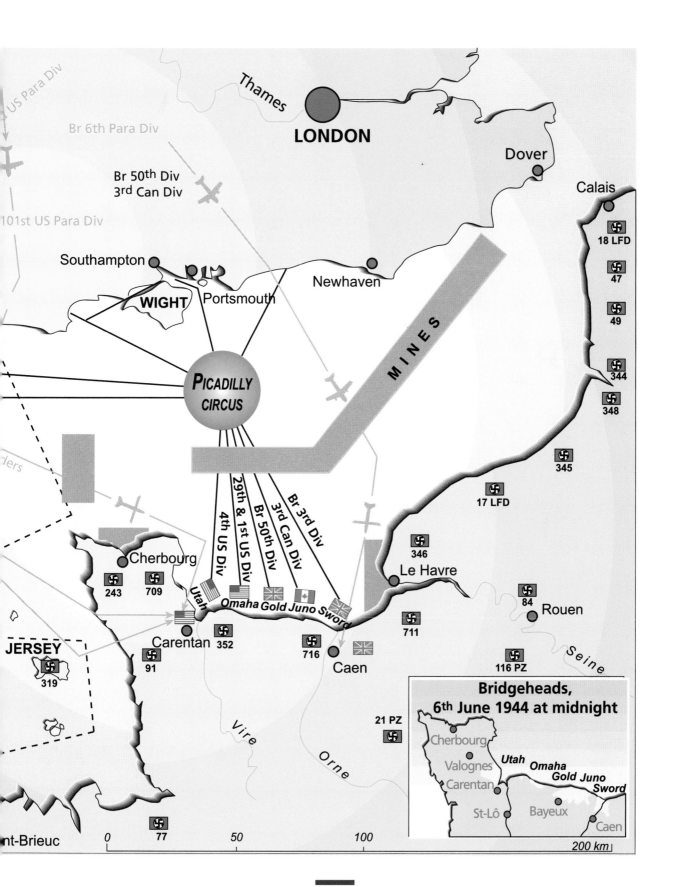

US Para Div

Br 6th Para Div

101st US Para Div

Thames

LONDON

Dover

Calais

🇩🇪 **18 LFD**

🇩🇪 **47**

🇩🇪 **49**

Br 50th Div
3rd Can Div

Southampton

Newhaven

Portsmouth

WIGHT

M I N E S

🇩🇪 **344**

🇩🇪 **348**

**PICADILLY
CIRCUS**

🇩🇪 **345**

🇩🇪 **17 LFD**

ders

Cherbourg

🇩🇪 **346**

Le Havre

🇺🇸 🇺🇸 🇬🇧 🇨🇦 🇬🇧

29th & 1st US Div
4th US Div
Br 50th Div
3rd Can Div
Br 3rd Div

🇩🇪 **243**

🇩🇪 **709**

Utah

Omaha Gold Juno Sword

🇩🇪 **84** Rouen

🇺🇸

Carentan

🇩🇪 **352**

🇩🇪 **711**

JERSEY

🇩🇪 **91**

🇩🇪 **716**

🇬🇧

Caen

🇩🇪 **116 PZ**

Seine

🇩🇪 **319**

Vire

21 PZ
🇩🇪

Orne

Bridgeheads,
6th June 1944 at midnight

Cherbourg

Valognes

Utah

Omaha

Carentan

Gold Juno

Sword

St-Lô

Bayeux

Caen

nt-Brieuc

🇩🇪 **77**

0   50   100

200 km

Utah Beach

Utah Beach

The Plain region, on the east coast of the Cotentin between Montebourg and Carentan, is an area of low-lying, humid country; a landscape consisting of hedgerows and marshes that become flooded every winter. Ever since the 17th Century, it has been predominantly given over to dairy farming. The wide sandy beaches that stretch along the coast rise up to a line of dunes that separate them from the marshes that are crossed by means of raised "causeways". >

• The Carentan marshes •

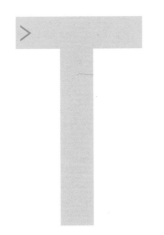

This sector of the coast lent itself ideally to an amphibious attack. Marshal Rommel was aware of this fact and stepped up the defensive system construction work there. As a result, the dunes from the Baie des Veys to Saint-Vaast-la-Hougue were studded with thirty-odd "resistance nests", the "Widerstandnesten" (WN). Heavy batteries were installed on the higher ground inland, notably in Azeville, Saint-Marcouf, Morsalines, la Pernelle etc. Finally, in order to counter the risk of an attack by paratroops, the Germans caused the valleys of the Douves and the Merderet to become flooded, transforming a good part of the surrounding countryside into marshland.

In their initial plans, the Allies had not intended to land on the Cotentin coast. It was not before December 1943 that Eisenhower and Montgomery decided to add a supplementary beach, west of the Baie des Veys, to those already selected on the Calvados coast, so as to be able to capture the port of Cherbourg more rapidly. The place chosen, code-named Utah Beach (after one of the American states), stretched from Sainte-Marie-du-Mont to Quinéville, and included a roughly 1-mile wide assault zone down from the Vareville dunes. The general staff decided to drop two parachute divisions here during the night before the invasion in order to protect this sector. Their mission was to check the German counter-offensives against the beaches. General Ridgway's 82nd Airborne was to capture the important crossroads at Saint-Mère-Eglise and the bridges over the Merderet. The 101st Airborne, under General Taylor, was to deploy its efforts to take control of the access routes to Utah Beach. Between midnight and 3 o'clock in the morning nearly a thousand C-47 Dakota transport planes dropped over 13,000 paratroops over the Cotentin, the vanguard of the Allied armies on French soil. However, for the most part, the drop was undertaken in difficult conditions. Many

• **Insigna**
of 82nd Airborne •

aircraft, targeted by the FLAK, were in a hurry to get away from danger and so were flying too high and too fast. The paratroops often landed a long way from the drop zone they had been assigned, sometimes dozens of kilometres away from the planned sites. Many became lost, entangled in trees or stuck in the marshes; some even drowned there, with the result that many units were incapable of regrouping to carry out their missions. Fortunately, this dispersion threw the Germans, who were unable to calculate the enemy's strength and position. The result was a night of fighting in the Norman countryside that was as sporadic as it was confused.

In the morning, the paratroops took hours to regroup and to make a first contact with the leading units of the 4th Division, which had landed at dawn on 6th June on the shore at Saint-Marie-du-Mont. The following days were consecrated to cleaning up pockets of German resistance inside the American lines and to the extension of the bridgehead. Further south, the capture of Carentan made it possible to link up with the troops en route from Omaha Beach. To the north, the capture of the Azeville and Crisbec batteries were the major steps on the road to Cherbourg. ■

• Paratroops of the 101st Airborne •

• Insignia of the 101st Airborne •

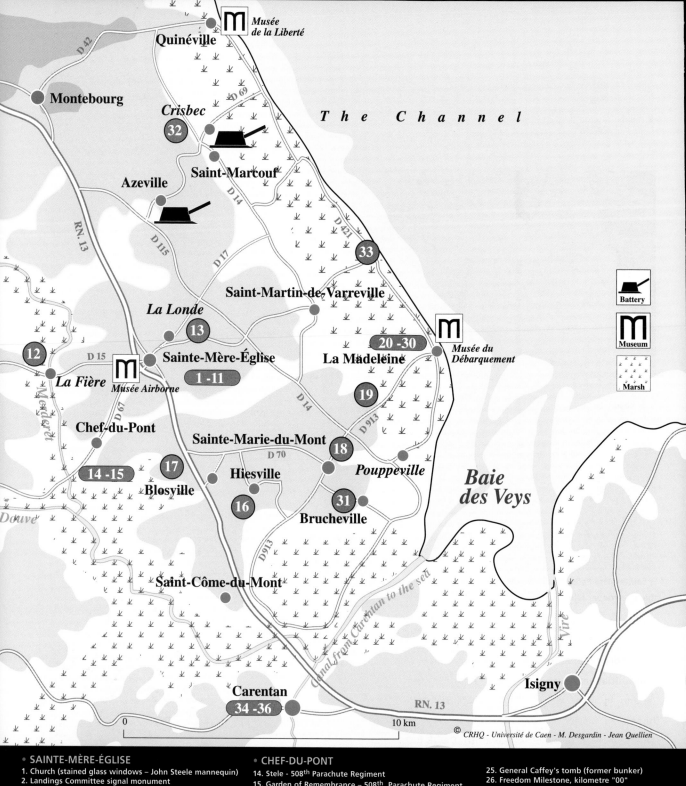

Battery

Museum

Marsh

- **SAINTE-MÈRE-ÉGLISE**
1. Church (stained glass windows – John Steele mannequin)
2. Landings Committee signal monument
3. Water pump (Fire-fight on the 6th June)
4. Stele - Alexandre Renaud (mayor of Sainte-Mère in 1944)
5. Commemorative plaque to four paratroopers killed on 6th June (rue de la Cayenne)
6. Freedom Milestone, Kilometre "0"
7. Plaque - "First town liberated"
8. Stele - civilian victims
9. Stele - Generals Ridgway and Gavin (82nd Airborne)
10. Stele marking the provisional cemetery N° 1
11. Stele marking the provisional cemetery N° 2

- **LA FIÈRE**
12. Monument to the American paratroops ("Iron Mike")

- **LA LONDE**
13. Stele marking Aerodrome A-6

- **CHEF-DU-PONT**
14. Stele - 508th Parachute Regiment
15. Garden of Remembrance – 508th Parachute Regiment

- **HIESVILLE**
16. Stele - General Don Pratt

- **BLOSVILLE**
17. Stele marking the provisional cemetery N° 3

- **SAINTE-MARIE-DU-MONT**
18. Plaques telling the story of 6th June (G. Perrault)
19. Monument to the Danish seamen

- **SAINTE-MARIE-DU-MONT, PLAGE DE LA MADELEINE**
20. Orientation table
21. Monument to the 7th Corps
22. Monument to the 4th Division
23. Monument to the 90th Division
24. Monument to the 1st Special Engineers' Brigade

25. General Caffey's tomb (former bunker)
26. Freedom Milestone, kilometre "00"
27. Stele - US Naval Reserves
28. Plaque - US Coastguards
29. "General Eisenhower's route" plaque
30. Plaque commemorating the 40th anniversary of the Landings

- **BRUCHEVILLE**
31. Stele - 36th Fighter Squadron, Aerodrome A-16

- **AZEVILLE**
32. Stele - 365th Fighter Squadron, Aerodrome A-7

- **SAINT-MARTIN-DE-VARREVILLE**
33. Landings Committee signal monument (General Leclerc's 2nd Armoured Division)

- **CARENTAN**
34. Landings Committee signal monument
35. Monument to the 101st Airborne
36. Stained glass window, Notre-Dame church (101st Airborne)

SAINTE-MÈRE-ÉGLISE

● Sainte-Mère-Église and its legendary mannequin representing the paratrooper John Steele ●

This little Norman village owes its current international renown first of all to its mayor in 1944, Alexandre Renaud who, through his writing and initiatives, was the public relations specialist lacking in many other villages where similar events happened during the night of 5th to 6th June. The village also owes its fame to Daryl Zanuck's famous film "The Longest Day". We particularly remember the tragic scene showing the first paratroops landing just after 1 o'clock in the morning right in the centre of the village. They belonged to the 101st Airborne, and had been dropped there by mistake. Unluckily for them, part of the population, which had been roused by the alarm bell, was busy fighting a fire that had flared up shortly beforehand. The German patrol supervising the operation reacted swiftly. A few Americans were killed, and some others managed to escape as best they could. More waves of paratroops, belonging to the 82nd Division, were to follow and receive an even more terrible welcome, as the whole garrison had by then been readied. Several perished before they even touched the ground.

The church square is obviously the village's main tourist attraction. A mannequin representing the legendary John Steele, whose parachute caught on the balusters, hangs from the belfry. Inside the building there are stained glass windows where profane, military imagery meets the sacred : one represents the archangel Saint Michael (patron saint of paratroopers) killing the nazi dragon ; the other depicts the virgin Mary surrounded by a host of paratroopers. Near the apse, in the shade of the trees on the square, the venerable old hand pump that was used to fight the fire on the night of 6th June has been piously preserved. Not far from there is the airborne troops' Museum, in the garden of the house that was ravaged by flames that night.

● The Liberation stained glass window ●

• Paratroops attempting to dislodge a sniper in the belfry in Sainte-Mère-Église •

is now conserved in the town hall. Less contentious, alas!, is the plaque to the memory of the civilian victims that bears the names of the locals killed during the liberation, notably by the German artillery fire during the morning and afternoon of 6th June. The fighting continued around the little town, which was threatened by the counter-offensives of both factions. The plaque on one of the houses in the Rue de la Cayenne that honours the memory of four paratroopers killed by a shell on 6th June around five in the afternoon bears witness to the fact. Close to the town, two stelae indicate the location of the cemeteries (a third is situated in Blosville) where the bodies of 14,000 GIs killed in Normandy were provisionally buried, before being repatriated to the United States or transferred to Colleville-sur-Mer. ∎

In Sainte-Mère-Église everything is nowadays organised around the memory of the landings and of the events of the night of 5th to 6th June. The visitor will discover the Rue du General Gavin, the Hotel du 6 Juin, the Le Dakota restaurant, Rue Eisenhower, the John Steele Hotel...

The different commemorative monuments grouped in front of the Town Hall merit some explanation. On either side of the milestone marking kilometre "0" on the Road to Freedom, two plaques (in French and in English) affirm that Sainte-Mère-Église was the first town on the western front to be liberated by the Allies, which is manifestly incorrect (without wishing to rumple local self-esteem) as the 3rd Battalion of Lieutenant-Colonel Edward Krause's 505th Parachute Regiment only took control of the area at about half past four in the morning, whereas Ranville, in the Calvados, had fallen to the British two hours earlier. Be that as it may, the American flag hoist for the occasion

• Milestone "0" on the Road to Freedom •

Milestone "0", inaugurated in September 1947, symbolically marks the start of the Road to Freedom that the American armies drove through France in 1944. Freedom milestones line both the branch that leads to Cherbourg, and the main route that runs through Avranches, Chartres, Fontainebleau, Reims, Verdun etc. and continues 1142 km (713 miles) to Bastogne in Belgium.

• Sainte-Mère-Église at a glance •

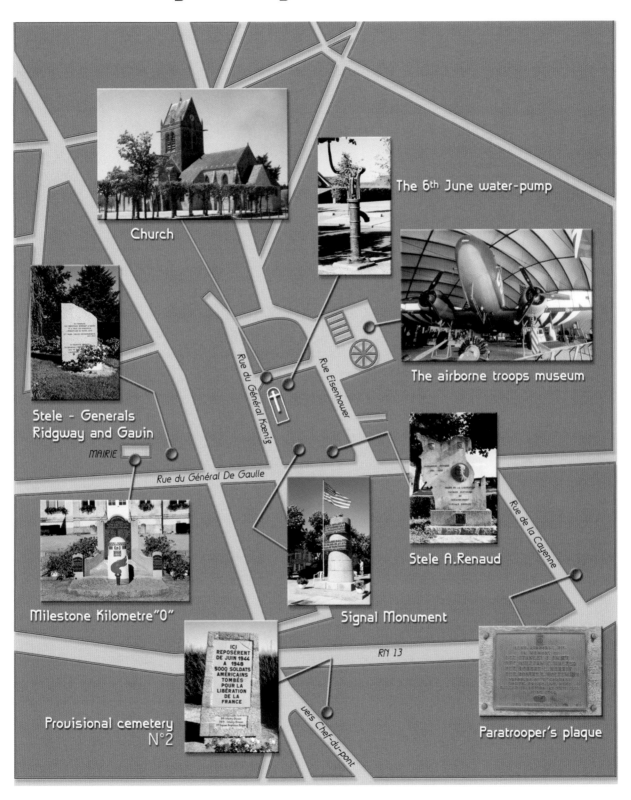

Church

The 6th June water-pump

The airborne troops museum

Stele - Generals
Ridgway and Gavin

MAIRIE

Rue du Général Kœnig

Rue Eisenhower

Rue du Général De Gaulle

Rue de la Cayenne

Milestone Kilometre"0"

Signal Monument

Stele A.Renaud

RN 13

ICI
REPOSÈRENT
DE JUIN 1944
A 1948
5000 SOLDATS
AMÉRICAINS
TOMBÉS
POUR LA
LIBÉRATION
DE LA
FRANCE

Provisional cemetery
N°2

Vers Chef-du-pont

Paratrooper's plaque

THE BRIDGE AT LA FIÈRE

From 6th to 9th June the bridge at La Fière and the raised causeway across the flooded valley of the Merderet were the scene of violent clashes. For the paratroops of the 82nd Airborne, it was both a matter of holding the crossing to prevent the adversary from marching on Sainte-Mère-Église and getting a foothold on the opposite bank, so as to link up with their comrades who were stuck on the other side of the river, still scattered and isolated behind enemy lines. For four days they had to hold out against murderous artillery fire and repel several German attempts, which were made with armoured support, before being able to begin their push towards Cauquigny. In 1997, a memorial paying tribute to the memory of the American airborne troops was erected on the rising slope near the bridge at La Fière. The key element is "Iron Mike", an imposing statue of a determined paratrooper, a replica of the one at the infantry training college in Fort Benning in the USA. A plaque set by the veterans of the 508th Regiment of the 82nd Airborne recalls the death of 336 of their comrades during the Battle of Normandy, and the wounding or disappearance of 825 others. ∎

• "Pont de la Fière" •

CHEF-DU-PONT

Along with the one at La Fière, the bridge crossing the Merderet on the road out of the village of Chef-du-Pont was the only way across the river in the drop zone. Because of this, its capture was one of the priorities assigned to the men of the 82nd Airborne.

As German resistance was particularly vigorous, it was not captured until 9th June, after heavy losses. Near the bridge, there is a stele dedicated to the combatants of the 508th Parachute Regiment and, on the other side of the road, a small garden of remembrance has been created at the instigation of the unit's veterans. ∎

HIESVILLE

• A crashed Waco glider •

A hundred or so Waco gliders carrying reinforcements, jeeps, 57-mm guns, munitions and various different types of supplies for the paratroops were dropped at four in the morning during the night of 5th to 6th June. This was a first attempt and the experiment resulted in many accidents, many of the aircraft crashing into hedges. This was the fate that befell the glider carrying General Don Pratt, second-in-command of the 101st Airborne, who was killed outright, his neck broken. He had the sad privilege of being the first General the Allies lost in the Battle of Normandy. A stele has been set up not far from the pasture where the accident happened. Other gliders landed during the evening of 6th June and the morrow, in conditions that were often no less dramatic. ∎

• Stele - General Don Pratt •

• Construction of the La Londe site •

LA LONDE

On the little road from Sainte-Mère to Beuzeville (D17) in the hamlet of La Londe, at the edge of a field, a stele recalls the establishment here of one of the first American airfields in Normandy in 1944. The construction work on the A-6 aerodrome started on 7th June. The runway, which was 1,800 metres (1,962 yards) long, went into service on the 12th, and was used until the end of July by the 371st Fighter Squadron, equipped with P-47 Thunderbolts. The whole set-up covered about 100 hectares (250 acres). The Americans built thirty such airfields in Normandy, most of which were in the Cotentin or the Bessin. They enabled squadrons of fighters and fighter-bombers to give vital support to the troops on the ground and played a crucial role in the Battle of Normandy. ∎

Sainte-Marie-du-Mont

The village of Sainte-Marie-du-Mont was liberated during the morning of 6th June by the paratroops of the 101st Airborne. A dozen panels on the houses on the square in front of the church recount the events of that night in anecdotal form. The texts were written by the writer Gilles Perrault, a local citizen. Along the road that leads from Sainte-Marie-du-Mont to the sea, there is a monument dedicated to the memory of the 800 Danish seamen who took part in the invasion. They were members of the crews who decided to sail for Britain with their ships to continue the struggle when the Germans invaded their country in April 1940.

Sainte-Marie-du-Mont owes its fame primarily to its beach "La Madeleine", three miles from the village, and universally known nowadays by its code-name Utah Beach. The 8th Regiment of General Barton's 4th Division landed here at 0630 hours, with support from amphibious tanks. It landed about a mile and a half south of the

• Sainte-Marie-du-Mont / La Madeleine at a glance •

Stele- 90th US Infantry Division

Monument to the 1st Engineers' Brigade

Milestone "00"

Monument erected
by the Americain government in 1984

Monumentto the 4th US Division

intended place. This was a providential error, as the German defences were considerably weaker here. The barges were swept down the coast to their port side by the coastal currents and landed opposite the WN 5, which had been severely damaged by the preliminary bombardments, and put up merely token resistance. The beach was rapidly cleared of the obstacles littering it by the engineers, and the main body of troops was able to land unhindered, in spite of sporadic firing from the battery at Crisbec, before heading inland to establish contact with

• 50-mm gun •

the paratroops. The 4th Division lost (killed, wounded and disappeared) no more than 200 men on 6th June. Between D-Day and the end of the month of October 1944, 836,000 men 220,000 vehicles and 725,000 tonnes of supplies were landed on the beaches between Sainte-Marie-du-Mont and Saint-Martin-de Varreville.

Around the Utah Beach Museum, a large number of monuments have been erected in tribute to the various units that took part in the landings, particularly the 4th and 90th Divisions. On the occasion of the 40th anniversary of the invasion, the American government had an 8-metre-high column of granite erected here. It bears the inscription: "The United States in a homage of profound gratitude to its sons who gave their lives for the liberation of these beaches on 6th June 1944". The memorial to the 1st Special Engineer Brigade, the oldest edifice on the site, was inaugurated shortly after the liberation by Colonel Caffey, the unit's commander. It stands over one of the former WN 5 blockhouses, which now houses a memorial crypt. This same Colonel Caffey was the instigator of the sixty-odd special signposts that are dedicated to the memory of those of his men who died in combat, and whose names have been given to various roads around Utah Beach.

The visitor who has already seen the Milestone "0" at Sainte-Mère-Eglise, marking the start of the Road to Freedom, may be surprised to discover the Milestone "00" at Utah Beach. After lengthy polemics adding to the already ancient rivalry between the two communes, the municipal council of Sainte-Marie-du-Mont, considering that the liberation of France had in fact started on its beach and not at Sainte-Mère-Eglise, decided to erect a second milestone, also inaugurated in September 1947. ■

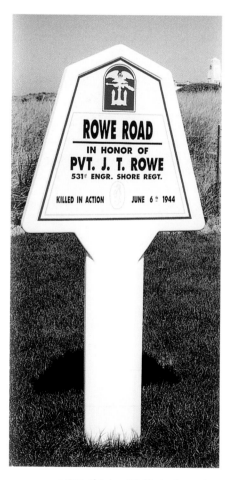

• One of Colonel Caffey's signposts •

CARENTAN

On 9th June, the 101st Airborne launched an offensive in the direction of Carentan, whose capture would enable them to link up with the troops coming from Omaha, who had just captured Isigny. Attacking from Saint-Côme-du-Mont, the paratroops had no choice other than to take the Route Nationale 13, the only way through the flooded marshes around the river Douve. The "Battle of the Carentan Causeway" lasted three days and was characterised by the bitter struggle to capture four bridges solidly defended by the Germans. The final assault was launched on 11th June from a small plot of ground whose location is indicated by a stele. The Americans entered the town the next day. It had been partially destroyed by the bombs and shelling. ■

• **The Americans entering Carentan** •

SAINT-MARTIN-DE-VARREVILLE

• **General Leclerc** •

The road that runs along the coast from Sainte-Marie-du-Mont to Quinéville, which is called the Allies' Road, is littered with very numerous vestiges of the Atlantic Wall. In Saint-Martin-de-Varreville, at the spot initially intended for the assault on 6th June, a monument indicates that on 1st August 1944 General Leclerc's 2nd Armoured Division, the first major French unit to join the Battle of Normandy and the liberation of France, landed there. ■

• **Monument to the 2nd Armoured Division** •

Close-up

The Crisbec/Saint-Marcouf Battery

Type H. 683 Bunker

The bunkers of the Crisbec battery measured 12 meters x 18 metres, and 7 metres high (40 x 60 x23 feet). They were covered with a slab of concrete 3.5 metres (nearly 12 feet) thick.

210-mm gun

The guns in the Crisbec battery were Czech in origin (Skoda). They could fire projectiles 210 mm in diameter weighing 135 kilos (300 lbs) as far as 25 km (15 miles). Their firing rate was between 70 and 80 rounds per hour.

A destroyed bunker

This bunker, whose covering slab has fallen in, was not damaged by the aerial bombardments or naval gunfire, but by experiments testing their resistance to explosives undertaken by American engineers after its capture.

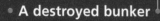

Apart from the fortresses in Le Havre and Cherbourg, the marine battery in Crisbec, situated in a dominating position 3 km (2 miles) from the sea, was the most powerful in the whole of the Baie de Seine. It was the cornerstone of the German defences in the sector. Its construction, which had been begun the preceding winter, had not been completed in June 1944. It was theoretically equipped with four 210-mm guns, but only three were operational as the fourth was undergoing repairs in Cherbourg. The first two were situated under colossal concrete pillboxes and the third, whose bunker was under construction, was ready for use, but uncovered. The battery had a garrison crew of 400 men and was a veritable entrenchment, complete with anti-aircraft guns and surrounded by a solid defensive perimeter consisting of machine guns, mortars and anti-tank weapons.

Because of the threat it posed to the Utah Beach landing sector, the Crisbec battery, along with the one on the Pointe du Hoc, had been the most heavily bombarded since the beginning of spring. During the night of 5th to 6th June, another 600 tonnes of bombs fell on it. The adjoining installations were damaged or destroyed, but the large-bore artillery was still intact, and able to open fire on the Allied fleet the following morning, although it did not succeed in inflicting much damage. At 0900 the two bunkers were knocked out by the American naval shelling. One of the guns, which had undergone makeshift repairs, started firing again momentarily on 8th June, before being definitively silenced. It was the third gun, pointing at Utah Beach, that opened fire on the landing troops and put them in very grave danger.

On the morning of 7th June, the men of the 22nd Regiment of the 4th US Division attacked the position, but were forced back with heavy losses. The assault was launched again the next day with massive artillery support. The Americans penetrated inside the position and began hand-to-hand fighting with the defenders, but the supporting fire on Crisbec from the neighbouring battery at Azeville, accompanied by the garrison's vigorous counter-offensive, halted the offensive in its tracks. A renewed attempt on 9th June also ended in failure. The Americans abandoned their objective temporarily and pursued their advance on Quinéville and Montebourg. Crisbec was isolated and surrounded but it still held on, in spite of severe losses in the garrison. On 11th June, the battery commander, Oberleutnant zur See (sub-lieutenant or ensign) Ohmsen, received the order to evacuate. During the night he successfully led the 78 of his men that were still fit through the American lines to the German positions, even though they were 12 km (7 miles) away. On 12th June, the Americans captured the Crisbec battery without a fight to find a mere 20 severely wounded soldiers that had been left behind. ▪

• A Bunker with its camouflage •

Firing command post •

The imposing command post has two levels and an observation turret. Inside the bunker, a small compartment has been prepared to house a series of panels with technical and historical information about the battery. Access is by the side of the edifice that gives onto the path.

• In 1944, this bunker was camouflaged to resemble a dwelling house •

AZEVILLE

Leaving the coast road, the visitor will discover the Azeville battery a few miles inland on slightly higher ground. It consisted of four 105-mm guns concealed in bunkers (camouflaged to resemble houses) that were set in pairs on each side of the road, and completed by munitions stores and shelters for the personnel. Because of the insufficient range of these guns (6 miles) the Azeville battery was unable to intervene usefully against the landings on Utah Beach. On the other hand, its garrison put up vigorous resistance against the men of the 4th US Division which tried to capture it as of 7th June. The garrison finished by surrendering on 9th June under attack from flame-throwers. As well as the bunkers, it is now possible to visit the system of subterranean corridors linking the different parts of the battery. ■

• The former bunker in Quinéville converted into a café •

QUINÉVILLE

The Americans captured Quinéville on the evening of 14th June. Many fortifications are still visible on the beach at the northernmost point of Utah Beach, notably a former bunker that has been converted into a café, and an anti-tank wall. A battery housing four 105-mm guns was situated on Mont Coquerel, the hill behind the town. Behind the Musée de la Liberté, a panel explains the nocturnal reconnaissance mission accomplished by a Franco-British commando unit in December 1943 that was part of the preparations for the landings. ■

M for useums

Musée AIRBORNE
SAINTE-MÈRE-ÉGLISE

The museum in Sainte-Mère-Église, whose foundation stone was laid on 6th June 1961 by General James Gavin, former second-in-command of the 82nd Airborne, is entirely given over to the American airborne troops. The first building, shaped like a parachute, contains a Waco glider used during the invasion to transport airborne troops and their material during the invasion, and has many showcases displaying weapons, documents, objects and scale models. In the second building, the main item on display is a C-47 Dakota of the type used for the parachute drops during the night of 5th - 6th June. Films and interactive terminals complete the information given to visitors.

Musée DE LA LIBERTÉ
QUINÉVILLE

The Quinéville museum is proud of its individuality, being a "museum without weapons". Its first role is recreating the daily lives of the French between 1940 and 1944 by means of photos, propaganda posters, tracts, newspapers, objects and mannequins in different situations. The lynchpin of the presentation is the reconstitution of a street during the occupation, with its shops and houses. A 52-minute film rounds off a visit to this original museum, which sees itself as "human rather than warlike".

Musée DU DÉBARQUEMENT
UTAH BEACH

Originally developed in one of the blockhouses of the WN 56, on the very spot that the Americans landed on Norman soil at dawn on 6th June 1944, the Musée du Débarquement was completely renovated for the 50th anniversary of D-Day. Besides a large collection of weapons and equipment (landing gear, guns, etc.) exhibited inside and outside the building, the museum also has scale models on display, one of which is a diorama of the site in 1944, many photographs, maps, period documents and objects contributed by veterans, and a 10-minute-long film made from cinema reel archives. The upper floor offers a panoramic view of the Cotentin and Bessin coasts.

Omaha Beach

Omaha Beac

T

● The Bessin consists of pa
has a long history of dairy
famous "Isigny butter" has
contribution to the region's
From the rocks at Grandc
Arromanches, the coast is
part lined by steep limesto
several dozen metres ab
The coast subsides seaw
villages of Vierville, Sain
Colleville to form a gap a
four miles long consisting
that slopes fairly steep
the beach to which access
small, high-sided valleys.

T he site, by reason of its topography, was easy to defend. There were no less than fourteen *Widerstandnesten*, for the most part implanted at the entry to the valleys that were barred by anti-tank walls and pillboxes equipped with guns. The Germans had covered the terrain with machine gun nests, mortars, minefields and barbed wire, so the place was not an ideal spot for landing operations nor devoid of risks, but it was the only one possible between the British sector to the east at Arromanches, and Utah, the second American beach on the Cotentin coast.

In March 1944, the beach was code-named Omaha, after a town in the state of Nebraska. Three months later, it entered the history books with the nickname "Bloody Omaha", because of the terrible losses sustained there by the 1st and 29th US Divisions of General Gerow's 5th Corps.

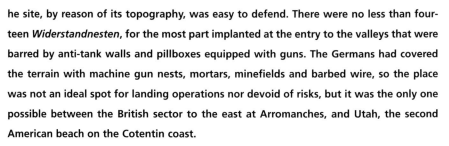

The first waves of infantry, which landed at 0630 hours, were welcomed by sustained machine gun, mortar and gun fire and were pinned down on the beach. The night's aerial bombardments and the naval artillery barrage just before the offensive had made very little impact on the German defences, which were largely intact and set about strafing the beach, strewing death in the ranks of the assailants. The terrible scenes at the beginning of Steven Spielberg's film "Saving Private Ryan" (1998) are without doubt very close to reality. To confound their bad luck, nearly all the amphibious tanks sank before they reached the coast, thus depriving the infantry of artillery support. For hours the situation worsened, The beach, which was becoming ever smaller as the tide rose, was cluttered with cadavers rolling around in the waves, countless wounded men and the smoking carcasses of machines destroyed by shells. The barges bringing reinforcements became impaled on or were blown up by the obstacles that the engineers, whose units had been decimated, had not had time to remove.

After an ordeal that lasted several hours for the American soldiers, the situation at last began to turn to their advantage. As they could not make it up the valleys, which were too well defended, the GIs managed to scale the escarpment, proof of their energetic bravery, at the end of the morning, and to penetrate onto the plateau in small groups, whence they could attack the enemy, whose resistance was weakening, from the rear.

On the evening of D-Day, the Omaha bridgehead was little over a mile deep, yet the Americans had achieved the most important thing. The operation, which had got off to an appalling start, was nevertheless successfully completed, but at what a price! Over 3,000 men had been lost (fifteen times more than at Utah Beach, including – officially – one thousand dead).

The 5th Corps, which had been given such a rough ride, rectified the situation in spectacular fashion over the next few days, making the most of the collapse of German resistance in the sector. The 29th Division broke through to the west, liberating Isigny on 9th June and advancing rapidly in the direction of Saint-Lô and Carentan, thus joining up with the Utah Beach sector. On its left, the 1st Division drove straight ahead into the Bessin, reaching Caumont-l'Éventé, twenty miles or so inland, on 13th June.

On site at Omaha, the very large number of monuments and stelae to be found along the remains of the Atlantic Wall, recall the awful sacrifice of the various units engaged in battle on 6th June 1944. There are two museums to be visited, one at Saint-Laurent and the other at Vierville. ■

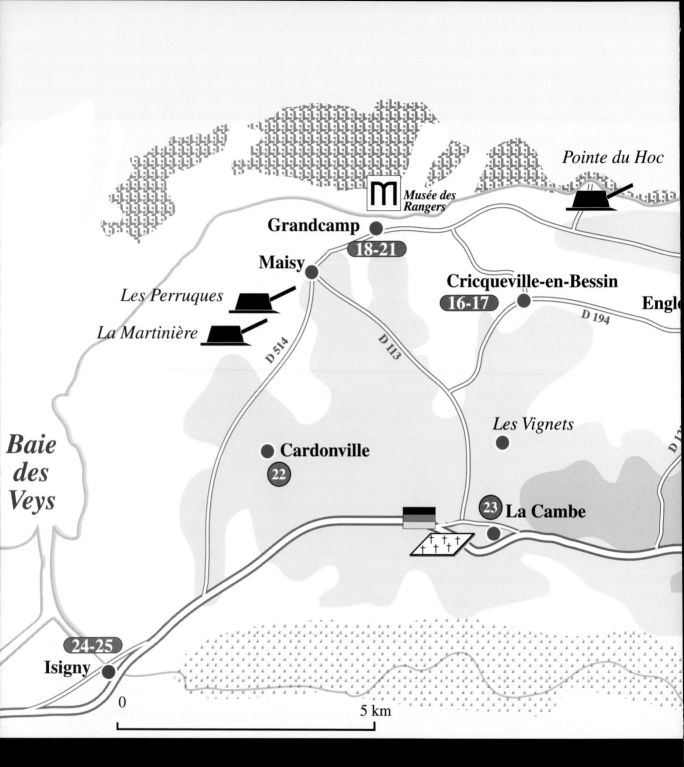

Baie des Veys

Pointe du Hoc

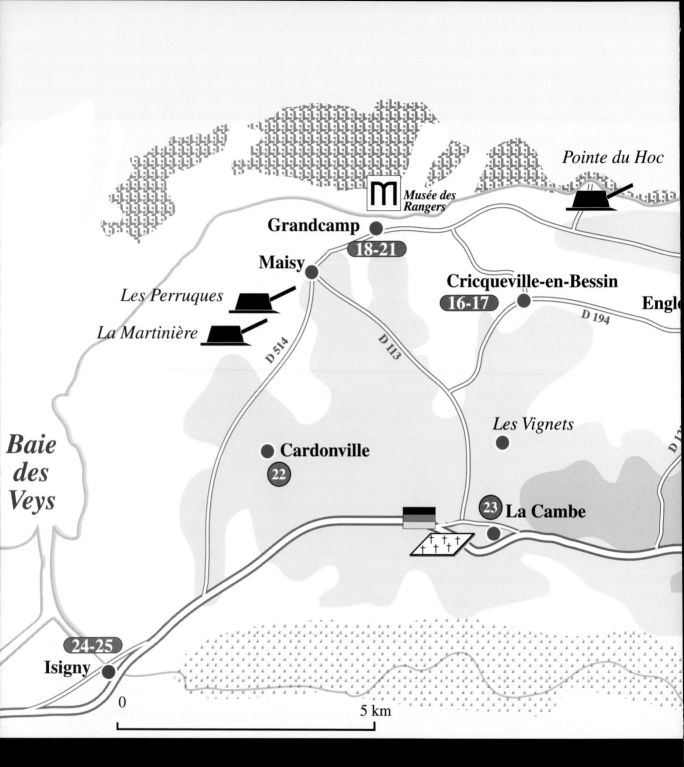
M *Musée des Rangers*

Grandcamp ●
`18-21`

Maisy ●

Les Perruques

La Martinière

D 514

D 113

Cricqueville-en-Bessin
`16-17` ●

D 194

Engl

Les Vignets ●

● **Cardonville**
`22`

`23` ● **La Cambe**

`24-25`
Isigny ●

0   5 km

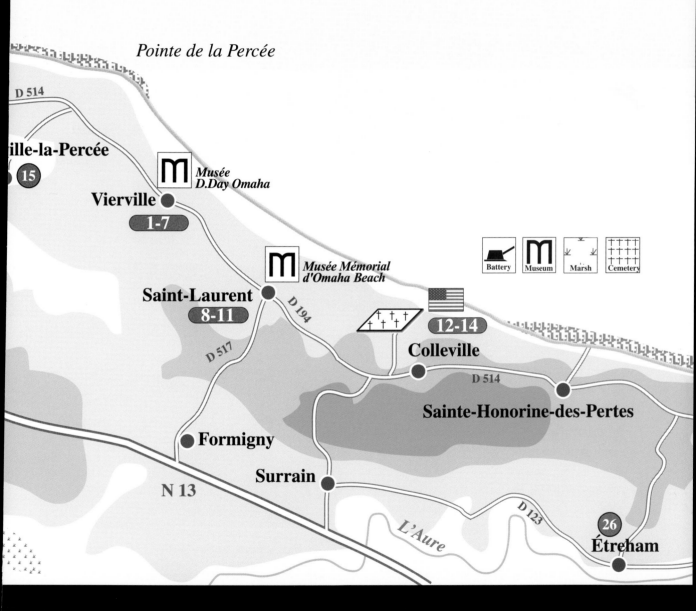

The Channel

Pointe de la Percée

D 514

ille-la-Percée

15

M *Musée
D.Day Omaha*

Vierville

1-7

M *Musée Mémorial
d'Omaha Beach*

Saint-Laurent

8-11

D 194

D 517

Colleville

12-14

D 514

Sainte-Honorine-des-Pertes

Formigny

Surrain

N 13

L'Aure

D 123

26

Étreham

| Battery | Museum | Marsh | Cemetery |

- **GRANDCAMP-MAISY**
  16. Monument to the *Guyenne* and *Tunisie* Bomber
      Groups (port)
  17. Frank Peregory space
  18. Rangers Monument (town hall)
  19. Stele recalling General de Gaulle's visit
      on 14th June 1944

- **CARDONVILLE**
  20. Stele - 368th Fighter Squadron (Aerodrome A-3)

- **LA CAMBE/LES VIGNETS**
  21. Stele - 367th Fighter Squadron (Aerodrome A-4)

- **ISIGNY**
  22. Landing Committee signal monument
      (General de Gaulle's visit on 14th June 1944)
  23. Stained-glass window to the 29th Division (church)

- **ÉTREHAM**
  24. Plaque - 1st US Division (presbytery)

VIERVILLE

• A jetty built on the remains of the artificial harbour •

Dog Green was the code-name of the assault zone at Vierville assigned to the 116th Regiment of the 29th US Infantry Division, supported on its right flank by the 5th Ranger Battalion. The losses sustained by these two units were the most severe in the Omaha sector, because of the murderous fire coming from the blockhouses guarding the valley leading up to the village, notably the pillbox housing an 88-mm gun on which the monument to the National Guard now stands. During the days immediately following the landings, urgency imposed the establishment of a provisional cemetery on the shelf between the beach and the foot of the embankment. Around 450 bodies were buried there, before being disinterred and transferred to the edge of the plateau, between Colleville and Saint-Laurent. The location of what was the first American Second World War cemetery in France is now marked by a monument, situated at the side of the road that runs along the seafront.

• **Monument to the National Guard** •

Before the war, the National Guard constituted one of the three branches of the American army, alongside the regular and the reserve troops. It was composed of militias recruited, trained and supported by the different states. Their mission was the maintenance of order in peacetime and to provide men in time of war. Several units were composed of the men of the National Guard, including the 29th Division that landed at Omaha Beach on 6th June 1944.

Symbolically, the monument dedicated to the National Guard has been erected on the blockhouse formerly housing an 88-mm gun (WN 72) that guarded the valley leading to the small town of Vierville and inflicted heavy losses on the assailants before being knocked out by a tank. On its three interior walls, bilingual texts recall the role of the National Guard during the two World Wars.

It has perhaps been forgotten: immediately after the invasion, the Allies undertook to construct two artificial harbours; one, at Arromanches, in the British sector (Mulberry "B") is now world-famous ; the other, in the American sector, has almost totally disappeared from memory. Yet Mulberry "A" was assembled off Vierville and Saint-Laurent. It had barely been completed when it was broken to pieces by the strong winds that blew up in the Channel between 19th and 22nd June. A few mere vestiges recall its short existence.

In spite of this fateful event, the Americans succeeded in landing impressive quantities of men, equipment and supplies (more than the British!) by beaching large transport ships with opening bows, the LSTs, or by means of big metal rafts, the Rhino ferries, and the DUCKW amphibious trucks that provided the links between the large cargo vessels moored offshore and the beach.

The organisation and control of this intense traffic fell to the 11th US Port, whose headquarters were established in the castle at Vierville, as we are reminded by a plaque affixed to one of the entrance gate's pillars. ■

• A religious ceremony at the provisional cemetery in Vierville •

• Stele marking the site of the 1st American cemetery •

• Omaha Beach at a glance •

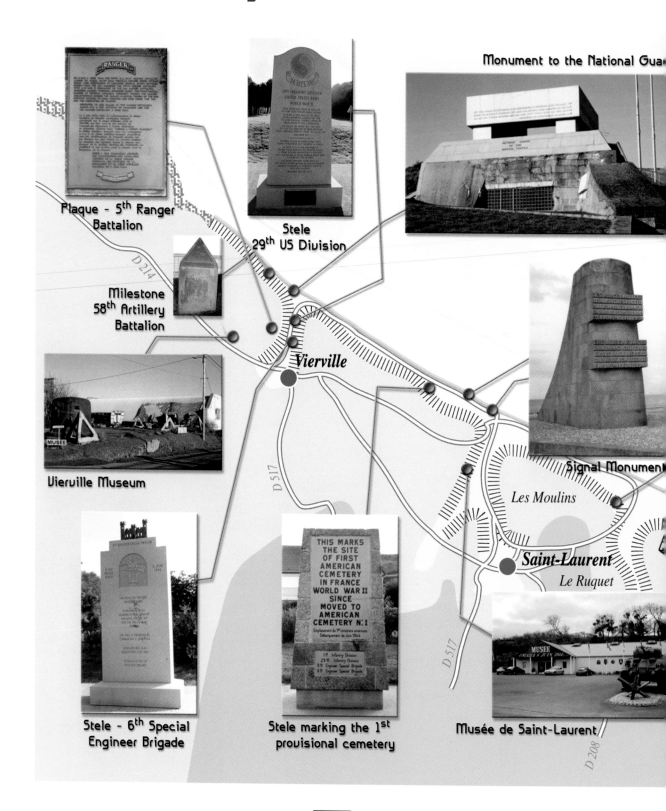

Plaque - 5th Ranger
Battalion

Stele
29th US Division

Monument to the National Guard

Milestone
58th Artillery
Battalion

Vierville

Signal Monument

Vierville Museum

Les Moulins

Saint-Laurent
Le Ruquet

Stele - 6th Special
Engineer Brigade

THIS MARKS
THE SITE
OF FIRST
AMERICAN
CEMETERY
IN FRANCE
WORLD WAR II
SINCE
MOVED TO
AMERICAN
CEMETERY N° I

Stele marking the 1st
provisional cemetery

Musée de Saint-Laurent

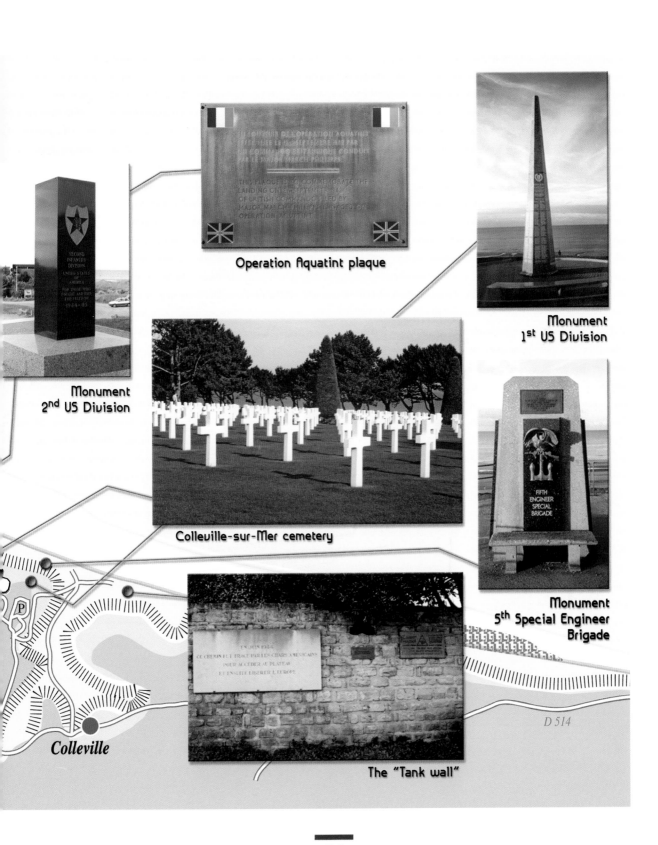

Operation Aquatint plaque

Monument
1st US Division

Monument
2nd US Division

Colleville-sur-Mer cemetery

Monument
5th Special Engineer
Brigade

The "Tank wall"

Colleville

D 514

SAINT-LAURENT-SUR-MER

A plaque affixed to the sea wall reminds passers-by that in the night of 12th to 13th September 1942, Saint-Laurent was the theatre of an Allied reconnaissance raid, operation Aquatint, which ended in disaster. A commando unit from the Special Operations Executive (SOE) consisting of eleven men carried by fast motorboat set out to collect information and take a few prisoners in order to interrogate them. This small group was rapidly discovered by the Germans and engaged in a nocturnal fire-fight lasting over an hour. Three men, including the unit's commander, Major March-Phillips, perished in the skirmish. Four others were captured straight away and three more shortly afterwards. Only Captain Hayes managed to escape. He was taken in and looked after by the local Resistance, who evacuated him to Paris, but he was betrayed and fell into German hands and was subsequently executed in July 1943.

Twenty months later the men of the 116th Infantry Regiment landed on the same beach, in the sector inappropriately named "Easy", opposite the "Les Moulins" hamlet, where they encountered ferocious resistance by the Germans that cost them severe losses. Here, an imposing signal monument was erected by the Landings Committee in 1959. Further east, at the entrance to the Ruquet valley, the Indian Head monument pays tribute to the 2nd Division, the first reinforcements to land there on 7th June.

Whereas the fighting was still raging all around, an airfield (code-named A 21-C) was hastily thrown together on 7th June at the edge of the plateau above the beach. It was functional that same evening and was used to evacuate the seriously wounded to England and fly in emergency medical equipment. ■

• Artificial harbour off Saint-Laurent and Vierville •

• The remains of one of the artificial harbour's floats •

• Monument to the 2nd US Division and blockhouse •

COLLEVILLE

The beach at Colleville was assigned to the 16th Regiment of the 1st Division, the famous "Big Red One", one of the most prestigious units in the American army. In spite of its experience, it was given equally rough treatment by the sustained fire unleashed by the Germans. Many men were only saved by the shelter afforded at the foot of the neighbouring cliffs. With vigour and courage a few small groups managed to make it onto the plateau up from Fox Green, thus contributing to tipping the scales of the terrible battle in the GIs' favour. Among the commemorative monuments in the Colleville sector, one is particularly memorable, the impressive obelisk dedicated to the 1st Division that dominates the beach, on which are inscribed the names of the men who fell on 6th June and the following days. Beneath it, the monument to the 5th Special Engineer Brigade pays tribute to the engineer units, who were so particularly put to the test during the landing on Omaha Beach while they attempted to remove the obstacles from the beach, under withering

• **Monument
to the 1st US Division** •

enemy fire, in order to enable the barges carrying reinforcements to reach the shore.

Today, in a calm serenity very far removed from the turmoil of D-Day, hundreds of thousands of people come to visit the impressive cemetery at Colleville every year, and stand in contemplative remembrance before the 9,386 impeccably aligned white marble crosses. A father and son lie beside each other. In 33 other cases, it is brothers who are buried together. 307 graves bear the inscription "Known only to God". The Normandy American Cemetery is the only Second World War American cemetery in Normandy, apart from the Saint James Brittany Cemetery in the Manche département (4,410 graves). Fourteen thousand other GIs bodies were repatriated to the United States upon request from the bereaved families. The soldiers who lie in Colleville are not only those who died on the beaches on 6th June, but also the men killed elsewhere in Normandy, whose bodies were first of all buried in provisional cemeteries then exhumed several years after the war and transferred to the symbolic site at Omaha. The cemetery was inaugurated in July 1956 and is built over a vast area stretching over 70 hectares (170 acres) granted to the United States by France. At the entrance to the central alley, opposite a large pool, there stands a limestone memorial of two loggias linked by arcades surrounding a 7-metre-high bronze statue representing the soul of American youth rising out of the waters. Behind the memorial is the garden of remembrance dedicated to the men who disappeared, lined by a long circular wall bearing the names of the 1,557 men whose bodies were never found. ■

• An aerial view of the American cemetery at Colleville •

L A CAMBE

• The German cemetery at La Cambe •

Very different to the cemetery at Colleville, and more romantic than conventional, the German cemetery at La Cambe is no less impressive. Over 21,200 bodies, most of them in pairs, lie in a clearing where occasional trees intersperse Maltese crosses in groups of five under little grave slabs that barely rise above the short grass. In the centre, an imposing mound surmounted with a large cross with statues on either side, marks the place where the remains of 296 non-identified soldiers were buried.

Other German military cemeteries, designed along the same lines as the one in La Cambe, were built in Normandy between the mid 1950s and the beginning of the 1960s in Orglandes, Marigy / La Chapelle-Enjuger (Manche), Lisieux (Calvados) and Champigny / Saint-André (Eure). They are managed by a popular federation, the *Volksbund Deutsche Kriegsgräberfürsorge* (German society for the care of war graves). In all, 70,000 German soldiers have been buried in the region. ∎

ENGLESQUEVILLE-LA-PERCÉE

On 6th June 1944, Colonel Rudder's Rangers mistook the Pointe de la Percée for the Pointe du Hoc, losing 40 precious minutes in attaining their objective in the process.

The Germans had established a large Kriegsmarine detection station called "*Imme*" on this promontory. It consisted of two *Seereise FuMO* 214 ("*Wurzburg*") radar units, a *Seetakt FuMO 2* long range device and a *Freya FuMG 80* radar unit. The Rangers' "C" Company, which landed at the western extremity of the Omaha sector, had been given the mission of capturing the station. After having suffered heavy losses, manœuvred along the beach and climbed the cliff, they got to the station only to discover that it had been wiped out by bombs and shells.

A few rare remains in the middle of a field indicate the former location of radar station "*Imme*". ∎

• The "*Freya*" radar unit, destroyed by the bombardment •

• Monument to the French Air Forces •

The Germans had established two artillery batteries behind the little fishing port of Grandcamp, intended to guard the Vire estuary at Maisy, in the hamlets of La Martinière and La Perruque. They were subjected to an aerial bombardment during the night of 5th to 6th June in which the French Air Force bomber groups "*Guyenne*" and "*Tunisie*", flying four-engined Halifax bombers, took part. A monument in the port recalls their participation. Grandcamp was liberated on 9th June by the American troops advancing from Omaha. General Bradley, the commander of the 1st Army, established his headquarters there. A stele in front of the town hall recalls General de Gaulle's visit on 14th June, after his visits to Bayeux and Isigny.

A museum dedicated to the Rangers has been established on the seafront promenade, and a monument in front of the town hall also pays tribute to them. At the edge of the town, on the way to the Pointe du Hoc, there is a space dedicated to the memory of Sergeant Peregory. ■

• The Peregory space •

On 8th June, the forward units of the 116th Infantry Regiment (29th US Division) were brought to a halt near Grandcamp by withering machine gun fire. Sergeant Peregory, who heroically charged the position armed with grenades and his bayonet, captured thirty-odd German soldiers all on his own. This deed won him the highest American military honour, the Congressional Medal of Honour. Frank Peregory was killed six days later near Couvains, north-east of Saint-Lô. His body is buried in Colleville cemetery. The monument also pays tribute to the National Guard, from which the 29th Division was recruited.

ISIGNY

• 19th June – civilians returning home •

Isigny suffered greatly from the fighting during the Liberation. In order to capture this small town, the Americans unleashed a frightful naval bombardment on the morning of 8th June, the aviation completing the initiative that same evening, resulting in the deaths of some thirty civilians.

During his brief visit on 14th June 1944, General de Gaulle delivered a speech that was both solemn and deeply emotional in the midst of the ruins of this shattered town. ■

M for useums

Musée D-DAY OMAHA

VIERVILLE

The Vierville museum, which is installed in a "Nissen" type former American military building, displays a part of the considerable personal collection of its curator, Monsieur Brissard. Apart from the displays of arms and equipment used by both sides, it is particularly interesting for its exhibition of original objects such as radios, optical components, Enigma encryption machines, sabotage equipment used by the Resistance etc. At the entrance to the museum, beside an reinforced shelter used in the coastal defences, there is a German 88-mm gun, a formidable weapon widely used in Normandy against both the Allied aviation and armoured units.

Musée Mémorial d'Omaha Beach

SAINT-LAURENT-SUR-MER

This museum, situated right beside Omaha Beach, presents a series of thematic panels telling of the Occupation and D-Day, as well as a large collection of uniforms, insignia, weapons and equipment used by American and German soldiers du ing WWII.
Outside the museum can be found a Sherman tank, an LCVP landing barge (Landing Craft Vehicle and Personnel), and above all an American 155-mm gun, "Long Tom", an item unique in Normandy.

Musée DES RANGERS

GRANDCAMP

Inaugurated in 1990, this museum retraces the saga of the American army elite unit, the Rangers.
A series of bilingual panels, including a large number of photographs, tells the Rangers' story from their creation in June 1942 until the fight for the Pointe du Hoc, which guaranteed their fame. In particular, the panels explain the training Colonel Rudder's men had to undergo in view of the extraordinary mission they were to have to accomplish on 6th June 1944. An exhibition of documents, objects and personal belongings contributed by the veterans completes the visit that ends with an 18-minute video projection.

Pointe du Hoc

La Pointe du Hoc

A few miles east of the small fishing port of Grandcamp, on the land around Cricqueville-en-Bessin, the vertical coastal cliff forms a promontory that overlooks a narrow shingle beach from a height of about 30 metres (100 feet) : this is the Pointe du Hoc.

The Germans had built a powerful artillery battery, capable of covering a considerable section of the coast, on this particularly favourable site. It posed a major threat to both beaches chosen for the landing of the American troops.

>

• The bombing of the Pointe du Hoc by the 9th US Air Force •

The Germans, who were aware of the defensive advantages of the Pointe du Hoc, built a battery there in 1942. It housed six 155-mm guns set in buried concrete vats open to the sky. These were guns made in France (1916 model) weighing 14 tonnes each and with a range of over 12 miles. In the spring of 1943, a firing command post was built at the very tip of the point. This commanding position enabled observers to scan a vast area. It was topped at the front by a heavy observation turret and camouflaged to resemble the structure of the cliff (this camouflaging is now gone) and was equipped with a powerful range finder set into a rectangular pit built into the roof of the bunker (at the foot of the present-day commemorative monument).

• A 155-mm gun in its sunken concrete vat •

The system was completed by the many concrete shelters, most of them buried, used by the garrison or munitions stores.

The battery, which was protected by a network of barbed wire, minefields, machine-gun posts and anti-aircraft guns positioned at each end, had a crew of 200 men, of whom 80 were gunners.

At the beginning of 1944, in conformity with the instructions given by Rommel, the troops stationed here did their utmost to provide shelter for the guns to protect them from attacks from the air. In the spring, two bunkers had been completed and a third was under construction. But, because of a lack of gun carriages, the cannons were still in their vats when the Allies launched a violent bombardment on 15th April that destroyed one of them. In order to save the five others, the battery commander decided to transport them secretly inland.

• Small storage spaces for munitions and material were set into the walls of the gun housings •

• Bunker •

The bunkers on the Pointe du Hoc (of the H 679 type) were about 15 metres (50 feet) on a side. The construction of each one required 600 m - (almost 2,000 cubic feet) of concrete and 40 tonnes of metal framework. The side walls were nearly 3 metres (over 9 feet) thick and had to support a roof two metres thick. Inside, there was a firing chamber, where the gun was installed and two compartments at the back of the bunker where the munitions were stored. The opening was protected by a tiered structure aimed at neutralising the shrapnel from enemy fire as much as possible.

• A corridor with security doors in a munitions store •

• Part of the cliff collapsed under the bombardment •

• The Pointe du Hoc at a glance •

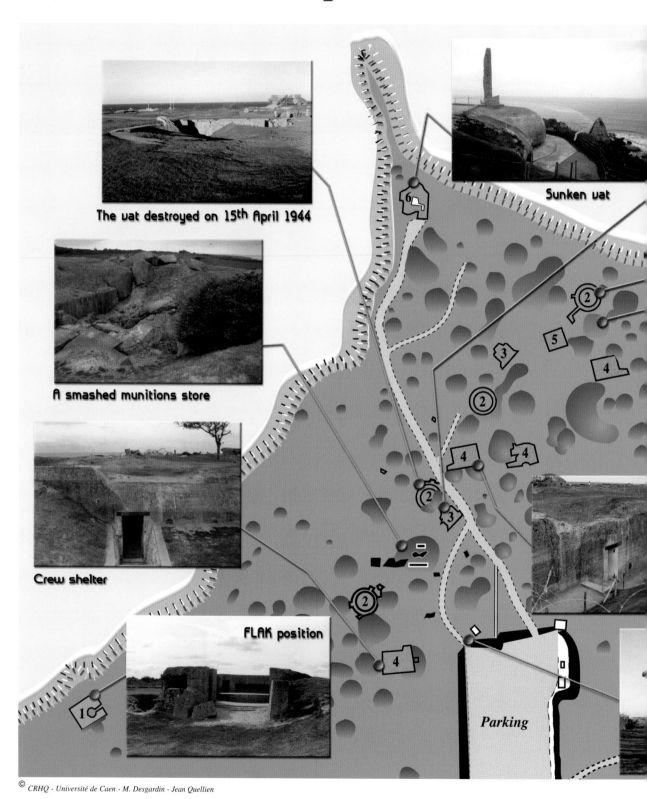

The vat destroyed on 15th April 1944

Sunken vat

A smashed munitions store

Crew shelter

FLAK position

Parking

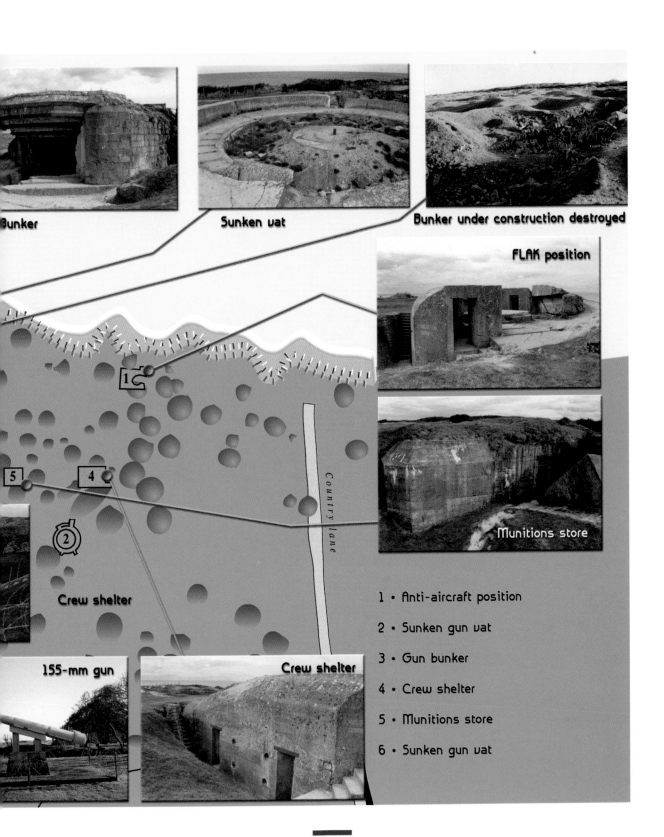

Bunker

Sunken vat

Bunker under construction destroyed

FLAK position

Munitions store

Country lane

Crew shelter

155-mm gun

Crew shelter

1 • Anti-aircraft position

2 • Sunken gun vat

3 • Gun bunker

4 • Crew shelter

5 • Munitions store

6 • Sunken gun vat

55

• Lieutenant-colonel Rudder's command post •

Aware of the threat that the guns on the Pointe du Hoc posed to the Utah and Omaha landing beaches, Allied strategists had decided to annihilate them. In spite of the bombardments that were going to be stepped up all through May and June, it was decided, to be on the safe side, to mount an assault on the position and capture it at dawn on D-Day, by scaling the cliffs using ropes and ladders.

This formidable mission was assigned to the 2nd Ranger Battalion commanded by Colonel James E. Rudder. The men of D, E, and F Companies, who were transported to the site in barges, succeeded in achieving the incredible exploit of scaling the cliffs in a few mere minutes, in spite of the very slippery rock face, ropes sod-

den and heavy with sea water and the fire of the defending troops. A ferocious fight, more deadly than the climb itself, started in a lunar, crater-strewn landscape.

A considerable surprise awaited the Rangers. They discovered that large wooden beams replacing the guns had been installed in the sunken vats. The guns themselves were discovered later by a patrol about a mile south of the Pointe. They were set up in a firing configuration in a sunken lane but seemed to have been abandoned; the patrol rendered them harmless, destroying their breech blocks with explosives.

Now began terrible long hours for Rudder's men, isolated on the Pointe du Hoc, deprived of reinforcements and subjected to a powerful German counter-

• Lieutenant-colonel Rudder •

offensives coming from all sides. They were only delivered on 8th June, around midday, by troops that had landed at Omaha. Of the 225 Rangers embarked upon this mad escapade, only 90 were still capable of fighting. Almost 80 of their comrades had lost their lives on this little corner of Norman soil. Their names are inscribed on a stele inside the firing command post. Another plaque paying them tribute has been set in the Cricqueville church.

The Pointe du Hoc is today one of the most visited historic sites in Normandy. That hundreds of thousands of people every year can today discover its spectacular appearance, sculpted by the explosion of bombs and shells, is due to the intervention of the Grandcamp tourist information office in 1945, requesting that the site be conserved in the state it was in at the end of the fighting, thus avoiding the landfill and the destruction of the bunkers that were undertaken in many other places. Later, this initiative was relayed by the Pointe du Hoc Committee, comprising local and regional figures. Since the agreement signed in 1979 with the French state, the management of these sites has been entrusted to the American Battle Monuments Commission. The worrying erosion of the cliff-face constitutes a real threat to the longevity of the site. Visitors to the Pointe du Hoc will find useful complementary information when they visit the Rangers' Museum in Grandcamp. ∎

• **The Pointe du Hoc Monument** •
The monument was erected in 1960 on the initiative of the Pointe du Hoc Committee. This large shaft of granite, which stands at the edge of the cliff on the former firing command post, symbolises the dagger the Rangers stabbed into the Germans' Atlantic Wall defences.

• **The Rangers monument at Grandcamp** •

Gold Beach/Arromanches

Gold Beach

Arromanches

● Gold Beach is the code-name given to the coastal sector assigned to the British 30th Corps, stretching from the American Omaha Beach and the Canadian Juno Beach. East of Arromanches, the cliffs give way to a low-lying coast behind which there is an area of marshland. General Graham's 50th Northumbrian Division was to spearhead the landings there, between Asnelles and Ver-sur-Mer.

>

● Landing at Hermanville ●

This experienced unit had distinguished itself in North Africa, notably during the Battle of El-Alamein, but it had also been active in France in 1940 and lived through the miraculous evacuation of the troops from the Dunkirk beaches. For it, this 6th June 1944 was something of a sweet revenge.

The invasion, led by the 69 and 231 Brigades, began at 0735, a hour later than in the two American sectors, as a result of the difference in tide times. As was his habit, General Montgomery ordered a massive bombardment of the German positions by the naval artillery, although the Air Force had already dropped tonnes of bombs on them.

The enemy resistance was concentrated at the two extremities of the sector, particularly in Asnelles.

Support from the special tanks of the 79th Division was to be needed to achieve their goal, after fighting that was very costly in men's lives, but in the middle of the sector the mediocre unit consisting of Russians that had been drafted into the Wehrmacht was overcome without difficulty, which facilitated the British breakthrough across the marshes, where they opened passages through the minefields using the "Flail" tanks. Thenceforth, the troops, with reinforcements from the division's reserve brigade, drove inland without encountering excessive opposition.

On the evening of 6th June, the British had landed 25,000 men and had control of a quadrilateral of about

• Insignia of the 50th Division •

6 miles by 6. For the most part, their objectives had been achieved. The forward units of the 50th Division had come within view of the RN 13 and had reached the outskirts of Bayeux. On their left flank, they had linked up with the Canadians who had landed on Juno Beach. On the other hand, on their right flank, whereas Arromanches had been captured, Port-en-Bessin was still in German hands and contact with the Americans had not yet been made, as a consequence of the awful difficulties that the latter had encountered at Omaha Beach.

During the days following the invasion, the British continued their drive south before being brought up short by the arrival in the sector of a formidable German armoured division, the Panzer Lehr. From that moment on, the front was brought to a standstill, along a line running from Caumont-l'Éventé through Tilly-sur-Seulles to Caen, until the end of June. Tilly was to be the scene of ferocious clashes.

• **6th June 1944 – British soldiers fraternising with the locals in Ver-sur-Mer** •

• **The 50th Division landing on Gold Beach** •

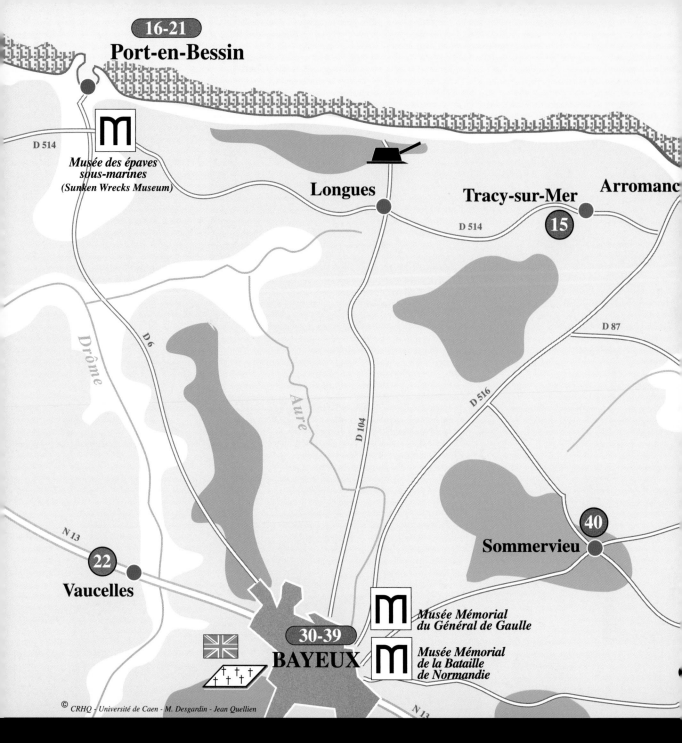

Musée des épaves
sous-marines
(Sunken Wrecks Museum)

16-21
Port-en-Bessin

D 514

Longues

Tracy-sur-Mer

Arromanc

D 514

15

D 87

D 516

D 104

Drôme

D 6

Aure

40

Sommervieu

N 13

22

Vaucelles

30-39
BAYEUX

*Musée Mémorial
du Général de Gaulle*

*Musée Mémorial
de la Bataille
de Normandie*

N 13

© CRHQ - Université de Caen - M. Desgardin - Jean Quellien

- **VER-SUR-MER**
1. Monument to the liberators of the village and to
   the 2nd Hertfordshire Battalion
2. Monument to the 50th Division's Artillery Regiment
3. Plaque on Admiral Ramsey's former HQ
4. "Sexton" motorised gun.
- **ASNELLES**
5. Plaque – Essex Yeomanry (seaside bunker)
6. Monument to the 50th Division's 231 Brigade
7. Monument to the 2nd Battalion South Wales Borderers
8. Monument to the call on 18th June 1940 (General de Gaulle)
- **ARROMMANCHES**
9. Stele – General Stanier
10. Stele – "Lorraine" Group (Free French Air Force)

- **SAINT-CÔME-DE-FRESNÉ**
11. Orientation table
12. Stele – Free French Air Force (General Fourquet)
13. Monument to the Royal Marine Engineers
14. Plaque – the "Liberation Bells" (church)
- **TRACY-SUR-MER**
15. 6th June stained glass window (church)
- **PORT-EN-BESSSIN**
16. Landings Committee signal monument (pier)
17. Plaque - N° 47 Royal Marine Commando (bunker)
18. Monument to N° 47 Royal Marine Commando (school)
19. "Essor" Monument
20. Plaque – the cruiser Georges Leygues (town hall)
21. Plaque – the cruiser Montcalm (tourist information bureau)

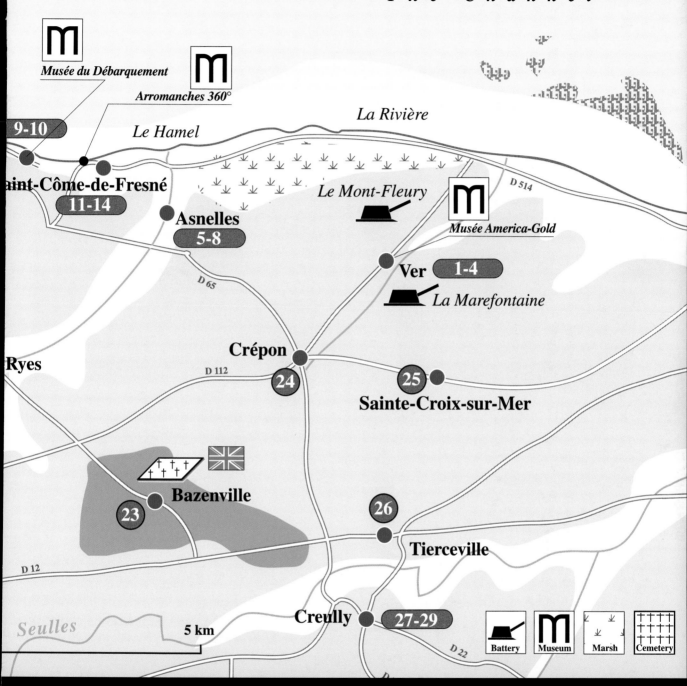

The Channel

Musée du Débarquement

Arromanches 360°

La Rivière

Le Hamel

9-10

Saint-Côme-de-Fresné

11-14

Asnelles

5-8

Le Mont-Fleury

Musée America-Gold

Ver **1-4**

La Marefontaine

D 514

D 65

Ryes

Crépon

D 112

24

25

Sainte-Croix-sur-Mer

Bazenville

23

26

Tierceville

D 12

Seulles

5 km

Creully **27-29**

D 22

| Battery | Museum | Marsh | Cemetery |

Ver-sur-mer

• **The Mont-Fleury battery bunker** •

The 69th Brigade landed on the shore at Ver-sur-Mer ("King" sector). They made rapid progress across the marshes. The main obstacle to their progress, the fortifications in the coastal hamlet of La Rivière (WN 33), was captured mid-morning, after a tank destroyed the 88-mm gun installed in a blockhouse that is still visible on the sea wall, which had been keeping the assailants at bay. The two heavy batteries situated near the village had been reduced to silence by the aerial and naval bombardments, and were quickly captured.

The one at Mont-Fleury, inland from the beach and equipped with four 100-mm guns, surrendered without a fight as its garrison was still in shock. The second, at Marefontaine, south of Ver, comprising four Russian 122-mm guns in pillboxes, put up little more resistance. A "Sexton" motorised gun is on display on the way out of Ver, on the road to Asnelles, at the intersection of the road leading to the beach (avenue Colonel Harper) and the minor road D514, near the monuments to the 2nd Hertfordshire Battalion and the 50th Division's Artillery. Not far from there a house, indicated by a plaque, was used by Admiral Ramsey, commander-in-chief of the Allied navy and the architect of operation Neptune, as his headquarters in Normandy. The America-Gold Museum is located in the centre of the village. ■

• **Monument paying tribute to the British liberators** •

• **"SEXTON" motorised gun** •

ASNELLES

• Blockhouse on the sea wall at Asnelles •

• Stele - the call on 18th June 1940 •

The 231 Brigade landed without too much difficulty in the "Jig" sector in front of the hamlet "Les Roquettes". But, in an oblique movement westwards, it ran into strong opposition. The fortifications in the village of Le Hamel (WN 37), which had been spared by the bombardments, inflicted severe losses on the British soldiers. It took them several assaults, support from armoured units and considerable reinforcements to clean out the position, only conquered after a pitched battle in mid-afternoon. A plaque, affixed to an imposing seafront blockhouse, recalls that the 88-mm gun housed there destroyed six British tanks before being put out of action.

On Alexander Stanier square, the monuments to the 2nd South Wales Borderers and to 231 Brigade are situated beside a memorial surmounted by a Lorraine Cross, evoking the famous speech delivered by General de Gaulle on 18th June 1940 calling the French to resist. It was in Asnelles, where he first reset foot on French soil on 6th June 1944, that Maurice Schuman, the former spokesman of the Free French and important post-war political figure, chose to be buried. He died in 1998. ∎

• 50-mm gun on the Asnelles sea wall •

ARROMANCHES

• **The artificial harbour in Arromanches** •

• **A general view of Arromanches** •

The assault on Arromanches came overland, not from the sea. Advancing along the coast from Gold Beach, the 1st Hampshire, with support from armour, launched their offensive from Saint-Côme-de-Fresné and took control of the town on 6th June during the afternoon. A stele, on the town's central square, pays tribute to General Stanier, commander of 231 Brigade, the "liberator of Arromanches".

Arromanches owes its world-wide renown to its famous artificial harbour, nicknamed "Port Winston" in honour of Churchill whose idea it was. Its story and its operation are fully described in the D-Day Museum that has been built on the sea front, on the very spot where a continuous flow of men, equipment and supplies surged daily in times past, on their way to reinforce the armies of liberation.

The remains of this veritable feat of technical prowess are perfectly visible today, from both the Tracy-sur-Mer and Saint-Côme-de-Fresné heights. ∎

• **Stele dedicated to the memory of General Stanier** •

SAINT-CÔME-DE-FRESNÉ

• *Würzburg FuMO 214 radar* •

• **Radar base** •

memory of General Fourquet, who was commander of the "Lorraine" Group. This unit of the Free French Air Force, flying twin-engined Boston bombers, shared in the bombardment of the German fortifications on 6th June. At dawn, one of these planes sank beneath the waves. The three crew members were the first French airmen killed during the invasion.

• **Orientation table** •

An orientation table offers a magnificent viewpoint overlooking the coast and the ocean, and provides substantial information on the artificial harbour. Nearby, the visitor will discover the monument erected in tribute to the Royal Engineers and the Arromanches 360° Museum, which houses one of the first circular cinemas to be built in France. A detour past the church in Saint-Côme reveals a plaque affixed to this venerable edifice informing the passer-by that the bells were set pealing as if they would never stop on 6th June 1944, in a celebration of the Liberation. ■

Climbing up from the town of Arromanches following a fairly steep footpath towards Saint-Côme-de-Fresné (to which access is also possible by road) and passing by a Sherman tank, the visitor reaches the top of the cliff to discover the remains of German defensive buildings. The only remaining visible signs of the former Kriegsmarine spotting station, which was destroyed by the aerial bombardments, is a large concrete plinth, the base of a Würzbug FuMO 214 radar installation. The esplanade on the plateau is dedicated to the

• **Stele dedicated to the memory of General M. Fourquet** •

Close-up

THE ARTIFICIAL HARBOUR IN ARROMANCHES

The remains of a floating causeway

The floating causeways

The floating causeways covered the half mile or more between the docks and dry land, and consisted of metal spans on top of hollow concrete floats, the "Beetles", which endowed the jetties with the capacity to adapt to tidal variations in sea level.

Jetties on stilts

The unloading docks were made of large metal platforms linked together by a series of intermediate jetties. Depending on the level of the tide, they slid up and down large 100-foot-high piles, by means of a system of pulleys and winches powered by diesel engines.

Phoenix caissons

These enormous hollow concrete caissons, weighing between 1,600 and 6,000 tonnes when empty, were destined to form the skeleton of the artificial breakwater providing shelter for the bay. They could measure as much as 200 feet in length, 55 feet in width and be as high as a 5-storey building. Once they arrived on site, they were filled with water by means of a system of sluices and sunk to the bottom. Some Phoenix were mounted with anti-aircraft guns.

The costly experience of the raid on Dieppe in 1942 convinced the Allies that any attempt to capture a large port by frontal assault would be in vain. Nevertheless, a large port was absolutely essential for Anglo-American logistics and the success of an invasion.

"As there are no ports available to us, we shall take our own," declared Winston Churchill. The idea of the artificial harbours was born. It was then a matter of putting this project, as inspired as it was complex, into practise. The task fell to Lord Mountbatten, chief of combined operations, with the assistance of Admiral Tennant and Commodore Hallet.

The construction of all the different elements necessary for the construction of two artificial ports, one destined for the American sector off Omaha Beach and the other destined for the British sector off Arromanches, began in England under the code-name "Mulberry".

The prefabricated elements, towed by tugs, crossed the Channel just behind the invasion fleet and their on site assembly, just like a gigantic Meccano set, began straight after D-Day.

Moored further out from the coast, semi-submerged cruciform metal buoys, the "Bombardons" constituted the first breakwater. The bay, which had a surface area of around 500 hectares (about 1235 acres) was fashioned both by old ships sun[...] "Blockships", and large concrete caisso[...] Dock on stilts linked to the shore by f[...] were established in the lee of this artif[...] Just when the construction of t[...] had been completed, high winds blew[...] from 19th to 22nd June. **Mulberry** disintegrated and had to be abandonec[...] elements were used to repair M[...] Arromanches, which was less badly dar[...] The latter was brought back into[...] the end of June an average 6,000 tonr[...] using it daily. This volume increased to[...] and 20,000 tonnes per day during July[...] Even if the role played by the a[...] at Arromanches has sometimes bee[...] (the Americans, who had been de[...] facilities by the tempest between 19[...] obtained better results at **Omaha**), technological feat remains one of[...] success of the landing operations. continued to be used after th[...] reconstruction of Cherbourg and was[...] in November 1944.

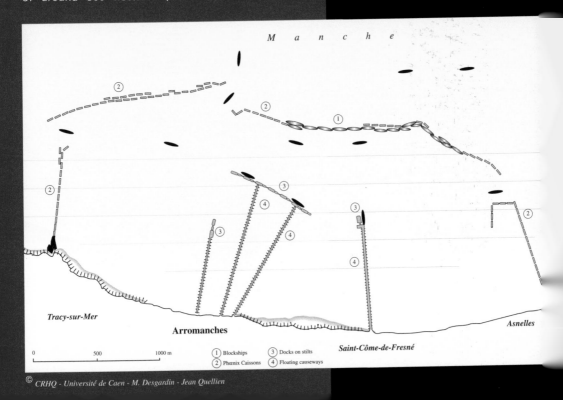

M a n c h e

Tracy-sur-Mer

Arromanches

Saint-Côme-de-Fresné

Asnelles

0   500   1000 m

① Blockships   ③ Docks on stilts
② Phœnix Caissons   ④ Floating causeways

© CRHQ - Université de Caen - M. Desgardin - Jean Quellien

PORT-EN-BESSIN

• The 47th RMC plaque on the Blockhouse at the foot of the Tour Vauban •

A plaque affixed to a blockhouse beneath the Tour Vauban and a monument near the school pay tribute to the men of N° 47 Royal Marine Commando, the town's liberators. They landed in difficult conditions on the morning of 6th June at Asnelles with the mission of advancing parallel to the coast and capturing Port-en-Bessin. They reached the town on 7th June, but ran into fierce German resistance, which only weakened in the early hours of the following day.

As did Isigny, Grandcamp and Courseulles, the small port, which was rapidly repaired, played an important role in Allied logistics before the artificial harbours were put into service. Port-en-Bessin was also, along with Sainte-Honorine-les-Pertes (in the American sector), the first fuel terminal on Norman soil, supplied by tankers moored offshore, before the completion of the submarine pipe line linking England to Cherbourg. From there, a system of pipes was used to transport the fuel needed by the Allied armies, whose consumption was considerable. This feat of technological prowess is celebrated by the monument "Essor", situated at the centre of the "Montgomery" roundabout at the entrance to the town, not far from the sunken wrecks museum.

Two plaques, one near the town hall and the other near the tourist information bureau, dedicated to the cruisers *Montcalm* and *Georges Leygues*, recall the participation of the French navy in the landing operations. ■

• Port-en-Bessin in 1944 •

M for useums

Musée DU DÉBARQUEMENT

ARROMANCHES

Arromanches is home to the oldest of the museums dedicated to the invasion, which is also one of the most popular and most visited with nearly 400,000 annual visitors. It was founded on the initiative of the Landings Committee and its president, Raymond Triboulet, the first sous-préfet in liberated France, and was opened in 1954 by the President of the Republic, René Coty.

A major part of the museum is, obviously, given over to the artificial harbour whose genesis and operation are described in a 15-minute multi-lingual film of period footage, photographs and superb models. A series of display cabinets and a diorama give a broad perspective on the invasion as a whole.

Arromanches 360°

SAINT-CÔME-DE-FRESNÉ

The Arromanches 360° Museum, unique in the region, makes use of the latest technologies, using the as yet rare technique of circular cinema screens. The spectator, situated in the centre of a projection space consisting of nine screens, is literally plunged into the heart of the action and becomes a witness to the events.

The film "The Price of Freedom", which lasts 18 minutes, evokes the different phases of the invasion and the Battle of Normandy. It is a skilful mix of archive footage and modern images, filmed on the same sites by means of a revolutionary technique popularised by the Futuroscope in Poitiers that uses 9 synchronised film cameras.

Musée DES ÉPAVES SOUS-MARINES

PORT-EN-BESSIN

Jacques Lemonchois was a member of the teams of divers who were given the task of ridding the Baie de Seine coast of the many wrecks menacing seafarers that had littered the sea bed since the invasion. Fusing a passion for history with the exercise of his trade, he salvaged and restored many tanks and other equipment that had been sunk, which are now displayed for visitors to inspect.

Not least moving amongst these relics are the personal effects of the members of the tanks' crews, sometimes even their private correspondence, that, miraculously, had been protected for decades by a coating of mud and were retrieved intact.

Longues

• The Longues Battery •

The naval battery at Longues, which was built during the first months of 1944, was home to four 155-mm guns protected by bunkers. They were situated some 300 yards back from the shore and were connected to the firing command post built on the edge of the cliff. Due to their range of approximately 12-miles, they were a threat for both Omaha and Gold Beaches.

Although it had been copiously bombarded before the landings, the battery at Longues was still operational and opened fire on the invasion fleet on the morning of 6th June. From the moment dawn broke, it engaged in a duel with the American battleship Arkansas, the British cruiser Ajax and the French cruisers *Montcalm* and *Georges Leygues*, before being reduced to permanent silence that same evening. The British troops obtained the surrender of the garrison without a fight the following morning.

A visit to the Longues site is exceptionally interesting due to the excellent state of conservation of this heavy battery, the fine restoration work there, and above all as it is the only one in the region still to have its guns. ■

• Firing command post •

• Bunker with its 150-mm gun •

72

CRÉPON

A picturesque bronze statue paying tribute to the Green Howards, representing a "Tommy" taking a moment's respite, has been erected in the town. They landed at Ver at dawn and had to repel a powerful German counter-offensive led by a dozen anti-tank guns as they advanced in the direction of the RN 13.

A plaque on the plinth pays particular homage to Sergeant E. Hollis for his various acts of bravery on 6th June that won him the Victoria Cross, the only one to be awarded on that historic day. ∎

• Monument to the "Green Howards" •

BAZENVILLE

• Stele marking Aerodrome B-2 •

In order to be able to give the ground troops sustained support, the construction of aerodromes on Norman soil was a high priority in the Allies' plans. The wide plain south of Caen, a flat and unobstructed area, was ideally suited to this project, but the doughty and lengthy resistance of the Germans outside the Norman capital prevented its realisation. The Allies were constrained to fall back on the Bessin country, a landscape that was less well-suited to the task because of the abundance of trees and hedges that first had to be cut down and flattened to allow the construction of several dozen airfields.

The Bazenville aerodrome (B-2), which was operational as of 14th June, was one of the first to be completed in the British sector, along with the one at Sainte-Croix-sur-Mer (B-3). A most original monument, in the shape of a Spitfire's wing, has been erected in front of the church in memory of the different squadrons of the (2nd Tactical Air Force) that were based there.

The Commonwealth cemetery at Bazenville was in use only a few days after the invasion. Of the 979 graves there, 630 are British and 326 German. ∎

BAYEUX

• General de Gaulle in Bayeux on 14th June 1944 •

• De Gaulle speaking in front of the sous-préfecture •

On the morning of 7th June, the British entered Bayeux without a fight. It was the first city to be liberated in France - the only one until the liberation of Cherbourg - and this peaceful bishopric became a hub of intense activity. The Allies opened a by-pass that went right round the ancient town, the forerunner of the present ring-road, to facilitate the circulation of the heavy traffic that was hindered by the town's narrow streets. Hundreds of refugees from the surrounding countryside flocked to the town, along with the many wounded, a multitude of Allied officers and soldiers taking time off, not forgetting the war correspondents, those dedicated customers of cafés. The town population suddenly doubled.

But, for several months, Bayeux also became the veritable capital of liberated France. It was here, to this little corner of territory freed by the fighting, that General de Gaulle came a few hours after he landed at Courseulles on 14th June to affirm the sovereignty of a free France. The enthusiastic welcome given him by the people obliged the Allies, like it or not, to recognise his legitimacy and to tolerate the presence of

the Prefect, François Coulet, who was charged with the administration of the liberated territories in the name of the provisional government of the French Republic. On the square that bears de Gaulle's name stands a column celebrating the event ; other monuments and plaques recall the day, as does the Charles de Gaulle Museum.

Right next to the Battle of Normandy Memorial Museum is the largest British WWII cemetery in France, with 4,648 graves. Opposite the cemetery, on the other side of the boulevard, is a portico-style Memorial on which are engraved the names of 1,808 soldiers whose bodies were never found.

In 1994, for the 50th Anniversary of the landings, the American Battle of Normandy Foundation and the city of Bayeux paid tribute to General Eisenhower, former commander-in-chief of the Allied troops, with the unveiling of a bronze statue, as imposing as it is realistic, in his memory. ∎

• Bayeux at a glance •

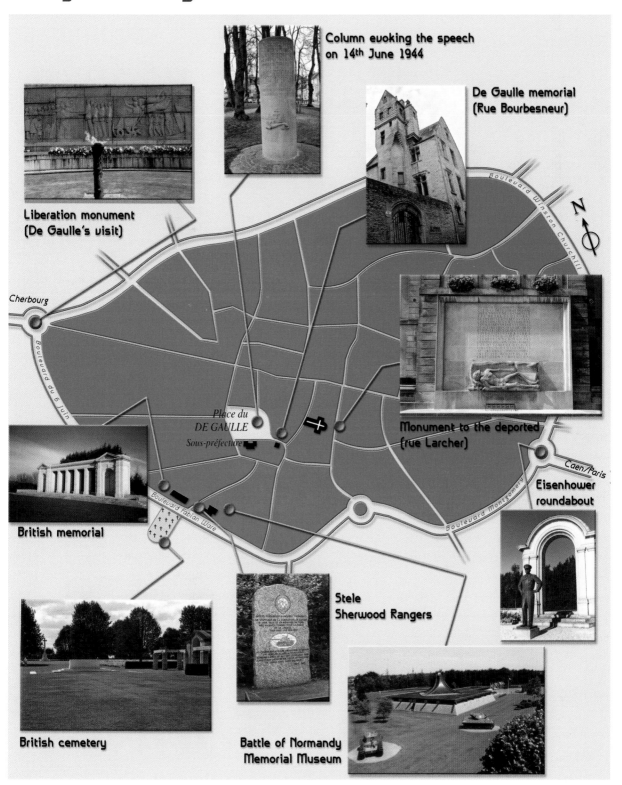

Column evoking the speech on 14th June 1944

De Gaulle memorial (Rue Bourbesneur)

Liberation monument (De Gaulle's visit)

Cherbourg

Boulevard Winston Churchill

Boulevard du 6 Juin

Place du
DE GAULLE
Sous-préfecture

Monument to the deported (rue Larcher)

Boulevard Fabian Ware

Caen/Paris

Eisenhower roundabout

Boulevard Montgomery

British memorial

Stele Sherwood Rangers

British cemetery

Battle of Normandy Memorial Museum

CREULLY

• The castle in Creully •

The small town of Creully, situated in the contact zone between the British and Canadian troops, was liberated during the afternoon of 6th June.

This mediaeval castle, which had already been occupied by the English during the Hundred Years' War, was home to a BBC studio that broadcast daily radio programmes covering the evolution of the battle in Normandy. As of 8th June, General Montgomery set up his famous tactical command post, a caravan in the grounds of the neighbouring Creullet castle. There, he received visits from various important figures such as Winston Churchill, King George VI and General de Gaulle. On the 23rd, he left and moved to Blay, west of Bayeux, in order to be closer to the Americans. ■

• The castle in Creullet •

• 12th June 1944: Montgomery receiving the Prime Minister Winston Churchill in the grounds of Creullet castle •

m for useums

Musée AMÉRICA-GOLD BEACH

VER-SUR-MER

The visitor may be surprised at this museum's name. In fact, its contents concern two distinct events.

The "America" part presents the first transatlantic postal service link achieved in June 1927 by Admiral Byrd and his crew who, because of the fog shrouding Paris, were obliged to land at Ver-sur-Mer.

The Gold Beach section is more particularly consecrated to the efforts deployed by the British Intelligence services during the preparations for the invasion, and the assault led by the 69th Brigade of the 50th Northumbrian Division in the "King" sector on the morning of 6thJune.

Musée MÉMORIAL DE LA BATAILLE DE NORMANDIE

BAYEUX

The Battle of Normandy Memorial Museum, based on the personal collection of its curator, Jean-Pierre Benamou, one of the most highly reputed specialists on this period of history, is without doubt one of the most complete of its type. Both inside and outside, it has an impressive collection of heavy equipment (tanks, lorries, guns, etc.) on display, and also numerous uniformed mannequins, equipment, light weapons, models, photographs and various documents very precisely illustrating the different phases of a battle that lasted over 80 days.

Musée MÉMORIAL DU GÉNÉRAL DE GAULLE

BAYEUX

The General de Gaulle Memorial Museum has been established in a venerable renaissance building, the "Logis des Gouverneurs" (the Governors' Residence), situated on the Rue Bourbesneur, not far from the sous-préfecture.

Apart from the presentation of objects belonging to him, copious archive documents, photographs and period film footage evoke the General's five visits to Bayeux, from those on 14th June 1944 and 16th June 1946 that were so decisive with regard to France's future, to that of 8th July 1960, as President of the Republic. On that occasion, in the same place from which he had spoken for the first time 16 years earlier, he declared, "How moved I am to return to this place, which is forever engraved upon my memory and which now is, without doubt, a historic spot."

Juno Beach - Courseulles

Juno Beach

Between the British beaches Gold and Sword, the Juno Beach sector corresponds to the portion of the coast assigned to the Canadians. This sector was occupied by good-sized coastal towns that had become coquettish seaside resorts towards the end of the 19th Century.

There were no heavy-duty batteries here, but a large number of smaller installations lined the shore at regular intervals. These housed anti-tank guns and machine guns that were often built onto the sea wall itself, in order to cover the beaches.

>

• Canadian troops landing •

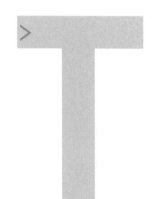

The mission to capture Juno Beach fell to General Keller's 3rd Canadian Infantry, with support from the tanks of the 2nd Armoured Brigade and backed up on the left flank by the British 48 Royal Marine Commando.

The sea conditions were to render the Canadians' task extremely difficult. The approach of the barges transporting the first assault wave was hindered both by the heavy swell and the presence of dangerous coastal reefs. When the landings began shortly before 8 o'clock, the obstacles on the beach had been largely covered by the rising tide and wreaked havoc among the landing craft. As they shuttled to and fro, many vessels were blown up by the mines set atop stakes driven into the sand.

On the beaches, losses were heavy as the infantry was often left to face the sustained fire from the German positions alone, the arrival of the tanks having been delayed.

But the Canadians were tough warriors. They were all volunteers, as the government in Ottawa, enlightened by the problems it had faced during the First World War, notably the resolute opposition of the French-speaking part of the population, had renounced sending men to fight overseas against their will.

Through sheer force, the first line of the German defences was eventually rent asunder, but the clearing of the villages was to be a lengthy business. The narrowness of the roads, (which were often blocked by obstacles), sniper fire, the persistence of pockets of resistance here and there all slowed their progress and caused worrying congestion on the beaches, which were shrinking as the tide rose and soon became clogged with a profusion of heavy equipment.

The forward units, however, lost no time in advancing inland, capturing Saint-Croix, Reviers, Tailleville, Bény, Basly, Pierrepont, Fontaine-Henry etc.

At the end of the day, over 21,000 men had been landed and the Canadians had established a solid bridgehead, seven and a half miles deep. Although they had not managed to reach the RN 13 and the aerodrome at Carpiquet, to the west of Caen, they were within sight of them. On their right flank, they had linked up with the British who had landed at Gold. On the other hand, to the east of Langrune, where the fighting was still raging as night fell, a corridor separating them from the troops at Sword was still in German hands.

But on 7th June the arrival of the formidable 12th SS "Hitlerjugend" Armoured Division consisting of fanatical young nazis was to bring General Keller's men to an abrupt halt. For over a month, terrible clashes multiplied between the Canadians and the SS outside Caen, characterised by the summary execution of prisoners (notably in the Abbaye d'Ardenne itself). The Canadian landing area, so far devoid of a museum, has now its own : the Juno Beach Centre, inaugurated in June 2003. ■

• Meeting between the people of Bernières and their French-Canadian cousins of the "*Chaudière*" regiment •

• The Basly monument •

• The 3rd Canadian Infantry Division landing at Bernières •

• Monument to the memory of the 20 Canadian soldiers executed by the SS in the Abbaye d'Ardenne, near Caen •

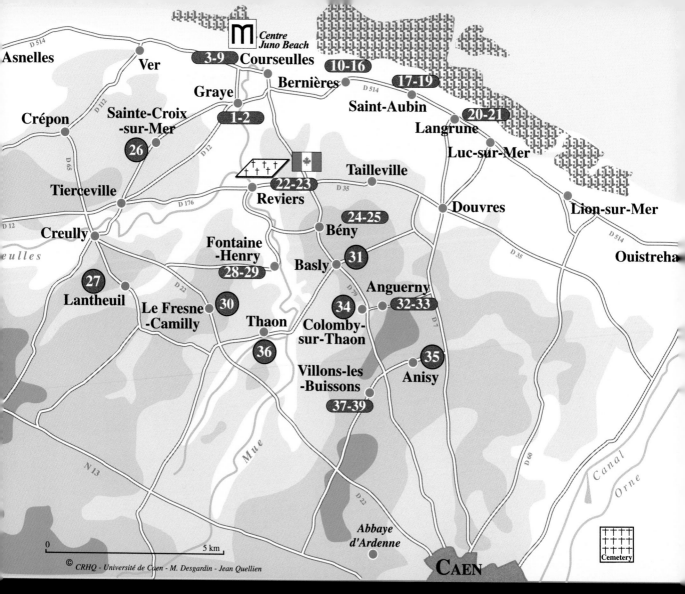

Map legend:

- Asnelles
- Ver
- **3-9** Courseulles — Centre Juno Beach (M)
- **10-16** Bernières
- **17-19**
- Graye
- Saint-Aubin
- **1-2**
- **20-21**
- Langrune
- Crépon
- Sainte-Croix -sur-Mer
- **26**
- Luc-sur-Mer
- Tierceville
- Reviers **22-23**
- Tailleville
- Douvres
- Lion-sur-Mer
- Creully
- **24-25** Bény
- Fontaine -Henry
- **28-29**
- Basly **31**
- Anguerny **32-33**
- Ouistreha
- **27**
- Lantheuil
- Le Fresne -Camilly **30**
- **34**
- Colomby- sur-Thaon
- **35** Anisy
- Thaon
- **36**
- Villons-les -Buissons
- **37-39**
- Abbaye d'Ardenne
- CAEN

Roads: D 514, D 112, D 12, D 65, D 176, D 35, D 22, D 79, D 7, D 60, N 13

Rivers: Mue, Canal Orne

Scale: 0 — 5 km

© CRHQ - Université de Caen - M. Desgardin - Jean Quellien

Cemetery

• GRAYE-SUR-MER
1. Landing Committee signal monument
2. Inns of Court monument (Brèche de la Vallette)

• COURSEULLES
3. Croix de Lorraine
4. Stele - "Nottingham Bridge"
5. D-Day and return of de Gaulle monument
6. Stele - First Canadian Scottish and the Scottish 15th Division
7. Stele - Regina Rifles
8. "La Combattante" memorial
9. Royal Winnipeg Rifles monument (Esplanade du Débarquement)

• BERNIERES
10. Bernières Landings Committee signal monument
11. Monument to the Queen's Own Rifles
12. "La Chaudière" Regiment memorial
13. Plaque - 5th Hackney Battalion, the Royal Berks Regiment and N° 8 Beach Group
14. Plaque - Fort Garry Horse
15. Stele of Remembering 1944 - 1994 (Bernières remembers)
16. Plaque - Journalists' HQ

• SAINT-AUBIN
17. Monument to the Fort Garry Horse
18. Monument to the "North Shore" and N° 48 Royal Marine Commando
19. Monument dedicated to the fallen from various Canadian units, the town's civilian victims and Maurice Duclos's Mission.

• LANGRUNE
20. Monument to N° 48 Royal Marine Commando
21. "Work of War"

• REVIERS
22. Plaque - Ottowa Cameron Highlanders (cemetery)
23. Stele - Regina Rifles

• BÉNY
24. Stele - Aerodrome B-4
25. Stele - "La Chaudière" Regiment

• SAINTE-CROIX-SUR-MER
26. Stele - Aerodrome B-3

• LANTHEUIL
27. Stele - Aerodrome B-9

• FONTAINE-HENRY
28. Plaque to the memory of the Canadian who died liberating the village (church)
29. Monument to the Canadian liberators

• LE FRESNE-CAMILLY
30. Stele - Aerodrome B-5

• BASLY
31. Monument to the Canadian liberators

• ANGUERNY
32. Stele - "La Chaudière" Regiment
33. Plaque - Queen's Own Rifles

• COLOMBY-SUR-THAON
34. Monument to the "La Chaudière" Regim

• ANISY
35. Monument du Queen's Own Rifles

• THAON
36. Monument to the Fort Garry Horse

• VILLONS-LES-BUISSONS
37. Monument - "Coin de l'Enfer"
38. Monument to the Norwegian troops
39. Stele - Aerodrome B-16

 RAYE

• Remains of a Bunker that once housed a 75-mm gun •

On the left, the Winnipeg Rifles and the 1st Canadian Scottish landed at the dunes down from Graye without sustaining too much damage and rapidly secured the village, situated a short way inland. Only a detachment of Russian gunners dug into the Vaux castle sanatorium put up any resistance. Without hanging around to finish them off, the Canadians drove onward in the direction of Sainte-Croix.

Over the days following D-Day, several important figures crossed the sand on the beach at Graye, including the British Prime Minister, Winston Churchill, who Montgomery received on 12th June, and King George VI, four days later.

The Churchill tank that can be seen in the dunes, not far from the Landings Committee monument and the Lorraine Cross in Courseulles, has a singular history. ∎

• The Churchill A.V.R.E. tank •

This "Fascine" tank of the 79th Armoured Division, which landed with the assault troops, sank into a marsh behind the dunes at Graye. The engineers immediately built a metal bridge over it to enable vehicles to pass. It was later buried under rubble and disappeared for many years under a metalled road. In 1976, the village mayor decided to disinter the tank, in the presence of the two surviving members of its crew, and to have it restored.

COURSEULLES

• Monument to the Royal Winnipeg Rifles •

• Amphibious "DD" tank •

The amphibious "DD" was equipped with a dual propulsion system (Duplex Drive), which enabled it to move both in the sea (using propellers) and on land. The chassis, which was made watertight, was surrounded by a hull around which was attached a high skirt of pliable material that enabled it - theoretically - to float. But on 6th June, because of the heavy weather, many of them sank before reaching the shore.
This was the case of the tank "Bold", fished from the bottom 27 years later, restored to its original condition and dedicated to Sergeant Léo Gariépy who led the assault on the beach at Courseulles at the head of the "B" squadron of the 1st Hussars.

Courseulles, a small port renowned for its oyster production, was without doubt the most solidly fortified section of the Juno Beach sector. There were at least a dozen anti-tank guns on either side of the Seulles estuary, not counting the numerous machine gun nests and mortar emplacements, so the task facing the men of the Winnipeg Rifles and the Regina Rifles was a tough one. They acquitted themselves of their task, albeit with heavy losses, and were in control of the area by the middle of the morning.

• The beach at Courseulles in June 1944 •

M for useums

Centre JUNO BEACH

COURSEULLES-SUR-MER

Raised on the same spot where the Canadian troupes landed in June 1944 with the others allied forces, the Juno Beach Centre, opened on 6th June 2003, presents the partaking of the Canadians in the military operations as well as the war effort on the national territory during World War II. A place of memory and discovery based on an interactive approach, the Juno Beach Centre adjusts to every public and offers as well the possibility to discover the different aspects of modern Canadian society for a better understanding of the country, its culture and the values of its inhabitants. ■

• The Lorraine Cross symbolising General de Gaulle's return to France on 14th June 1944 •

Apart from the various monuments erected in tribute to Courseulles' liberators, most of which are located on Charles de Gaulle square or near it, several relics, including a "DD" amphibious tank and a German 50-mm anti-tank gun, recall the fighting in 1944.

From 8th June onwards, the port, reconstructed and protected offshore by a Gooseberry (a screen of old ships scuttled on site) was used to land men and equipment, sometimes as much as 2,000 tonnes per day.

It was on the beach at Courseulles that General de Gaulle set foot in the early afternoon on 14th June, having been brought from England by "*La Combattante*", a Free French navy torpedo boat that had been on the same spot eight days previously as supporting fire-power for the invading Canadian troops. From there, in the company of his closest colleagues, the General went about crisscrossing the whole bridgehead area with the intention of affirming the authority of the provisional government of the French Republic. The memory of this event is recalled by several monuments, of which the most spectacular and most recent is the immense Lorraine Cross erected in 1990 on the dune at the territorial limit of Graye beach.■

Bernières

• The large villa visible in the background of the 1944 photograph, near the signal monument •

Bernières found itself in the centre of the 8th Brigade's assault sector "Nan White". The Queen's Own Rifles of Canada Regiment suffered heavy losses before smashing through the German defences. One of the companies lost half of its men in the hundred yards of beach separating them from the sea wall. The famous "*La Chaudière*" Regiment that was composed mostly of French-speaking Canadians landed here, too, in the second wave. Their mission was to rid the village of the snipers lurking there. The locals discovered to their astonishment that these "Tommies" spoke French.

Because of the delays in getting the troops moving inland, the beach was soon blocked with men and equipment, above all after the arrival of a brigade of reinforcements. General Keller, commander of the 3rd Division, set up his HQ in Bernières around midday. The British and Canadian war correspondents chose themselves a hotel from which to send their first reports. Nowadays, the hotel has become a private house (N°228, rue du Régiment de *la Chaudière*) and there is a memorial plaque on its façade. Most of the commemorative memorials have been erected on the sea front on the Place du Canada, where the WN 28 previously stood. This system of defences, nicknamed "*La Cassine*" by the Canadians, was the focal point of the fighting in 1944. ■

• The Canadians suffered heavy losses during the capture of the *"La Cassine"* fortification •

• Commemorative monuments, Place du Canada •

• Monument to the *"La Chaudière"* Regiment •

SAINT-AUBIN

• **50-mm anti-tank gun on the sea wall at Saint-Aubin** •

Well before the landings, Saint-Aubin had been the scene of an important event. During the night of 3rd to 4th August 1940, two agents of Free France, Maurice Duclos ("Saint-Jacques") and Alexandre Beresnikoff ("Corvisart") began one of the very first reconnaissance missions undertaken in occupied France. Four years later, the men of the North Shore landed here, with support from the Fort Garry Horse and flanked on their left by the British Royal Marines of N°48 Commando. The assailants on this section of "Nan Red" were given a particularly rough reception by the German defences, notably by a 50-mm gun housed in a bunker that is still in place on the sea wall. Several monument have been erected near the bunker on the Place des Canadiens. On either side of the memorial to the memory of the North Shore, and N°48 Royal Marine Commando, two stelae resembling open books bear the names of the soldiers of various units who fell at Saint-Aubin, and those of the local civilian victims. They also evoke "Saint-Jacques" mission. ∎

• **Commemorative monuments, Square des Canadiens** •

LANGRUNE

• N° 48 Royal Marine Commando, which landed at Saint-Aubin, encountered severe difficulties in liberating Langrune •

The monument paying tribute to N°48 Royal Marine Commando was erected on the Place du 6 Juin at the very place where a group of houses the Germans had transformed into a formidable fortification formerly stood.

having landed in particularly adverse conditions to the east of Saint-Aubin, the British commandos' mission consisted in moving along the coast in order to make contact with Sword Beach. They were held up for a long time at Langrune, where they were obliged to fight road by road, house by house, before wresting definitive mastery of the village from the Germans on 7th June at the beginning of the afternoon. By then, only 340 men of the 630 engaged in the battle on the morning of 6th June were still fit to fight. Near the N°48 Commando monument, there is an original piece of sculpture by Dominique Colas, "Work of War", made using compressed weapons and military equipment. ■

• "Work of War", by the sculptor Dominique Colas. The monument to N°48 Commando is in the background •

Close-up

OF THE COMMONWEALTH CEMETERIES

The Stone of Remembrance

Each of these monuments, only present in the largest cemeteries, bears the inscription : "Their name liveth for evermore".

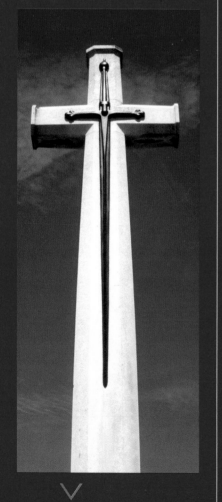

The Cross of Sacrifice

Aerial view of the Bayeux cemetery

• Canadian cemetery in Reviers •

The Canadian soldiers killed during the Battle of Normandy were for the most part buried in two cemeteries, one in Reviers (2,094 graves) and the other in Cintheaux (2,958 graves) situated between Caen and Falaise.

• The grave of soldier Ouellet (Reviers) •

Each stele is engraved with the emblem of the weapon or the regiment to which the deceased belonged. In the case of Canadians, this is replaced by a maple leaf, and a fern for New Zealanders. A personalised inscription chosen by the bereaved family figures beneath the deceased's name.

By virtue of a very ancient custom in the British army, the bodies of soldiers killed in wartime are not repatriated but are buried where they fell. Consequently, cemeteries are sometimes very small (47 graves in Chouains), and the number of Commonwealth cemeteries in Normandy is very high (16 British, 2 Canadian), not counting the several hundred graves in local village graveyards throughout the region. Another original aspect is the frequent presence of graves of soldiers of other nationalities, including Germans (a third of the graves at Bazenville).

The Commonwealth cemeteries all share the same general architectural design, established during WW1. The presence of trees, flower beds, pergolas and a border with flowers running along the foot of the graves give the impression of being in a garden as much as being in a cemetery.

The composition is simple and is organised around a wide central alley. A Cross of Sacrifice set with a bronze double-edged sword stands in all the cemeteries. Commemorative ceremonies take place at the foot of these crosses. Open-air altar-shaped monuments, the Stones of Remembrance, have been set in the largest cemeteries. Depending on their size, the Commonwealth cemeteries include one or two reception buildings in which are kept the register and the visitors' book, a map and a text describing operations during the Battle of Normandy. Each grave is marked by a rectangular white Italian limestone stele, with a slightly rounded top.

• Douvres cemetery •

Sword Beach

Sword Beach

* Initially, the landing sector defined by the Allies reached no further east than Courseulles. Eisenhower and Montgomery extended it as far as the river Orne. Thus it was that Sword Beach appeared to the east of Juno Beach ; it theoretically stretched from Langrune to Ouistreham.

Considering the risks weighing on a direct assault against the powerful coastal defences at Ouistreham, and the impossibility of landing opposite Lion and Luc-sur-Mer because of the coastal reefs, the site chosen for the offensive was a relatively narrow strip between Hermanville and Colleville.

• The battery on Ouistreham beach •

t was here that General Rennie's British 3rd Division landed with support from amphibious and special tanks. On the flanks, it had support in the person of the "Green Berets", two special commando brigades. To the east, the 1st Brigade, commanded by Lord Lovat, a Scottish nobleman never without his loyal piper, the famous Bill Millin, had been entrusted with the mission of heading left and capturing Ouistreham side-on. At the other extremity, the 4th Brigade (N°s 41 and 46 Commando) were to take Lion-sur-Mer and Luc-sur-Mer.

• Insignia of the British Commandos •

The 8th Brigade of the 3rd Division, which landed at a spot aptly named "La Brèche" (The Breach), succeeded in breaking through the Atlantic Wall, in spite of doughty opposition. It now fell to the 185th Brigade to make the most of the situation in carrying out a mission of capital importance: seize Caen before nightfall.

However, the overcrowding of the beach, resulting both from the disorder caused by the German artillery fire and the narrowness of the roads that held up the flow of troops inland, were already jeopardising the accomplishment of their objective. The resistance put up by the fortified positions around the village of Colleville, and the counter-attack launched by the 21st Panzer in mid-afternoon on the Périers-sur-le-Dan ridge, made the problem ever more complicated. The lack of decisiveness of certain high-ranking British officers, who were more concerned with consolidating their hold on the ground than forging ahead, did the rest.

When the leading elements of the 3rd Division finally drew near to Caen, in the early evening, it was already too late. They were pinned down by the defensive barrier established by the Germans. It was to take a month of unstinting and violent fighting before they could enter the city, which had been devastated by the battle.

Meanwhile, Lord Lovat's 1st Special Brigade had reached the Bénouville and Ranville bridges and joined up with the paratroops. ■

• N°45 Royal Marine Commando •

• The 1st Suffolk Regiment (3rd Division) landing on Queen White •

• The 21st Panzer counter-attacking •

• Stele - British 3rd Division,
in Périers-sur-le-Dan •

HERMANVILLE

• The Place du Cuirassé Courbet •

The British 3rd Infantry Division landed on Queen Beach, a sector principally situated in front of Hermanville. Whereas the South Lancashire did not meet with particular difficulties on Queen White, the same could not be said of the East Yorkshire which landed on Queen Red. Nevertheless, Hermanville was secured by 10 o'clock in the morning and reinforcements could start landing in their turn.

Offshore from Hermanville, and in order to facilitate

• The Hermanville Gooseberry ; in the middle, the Courbet •

operations on the beach, the Allies quickly established a Gooseberry, a breakwater constituted of old ships scuppered on site. Amongst them was the old French battleship Courbet (launched in 1911), which had fled to England in 1940, and whose carcass is still at the bottom of the sea. The French tricolour that was flying from its masthead today embellishes one of the town hall's walls. A stele reminds the visitor that when the commander of the Courbet, Captain Wietzel, reached land, he picked up a handful of French earth to take back to General de Gaulle. The precious packet is now kept in Colombey-les-Deux-Églises.

Various commemorative monuments have been erected in front of the tourist information bureau on the Place du Cuirassé Courbet. One of them pays tribute to the Allied pioneers who landed on the beach ... on 5th June at 2300 hours ; an affirmation that causes a few

• A Bren carrier in front of the Hotel de la Brèche •

historians' eyebrows to be raised. Near a horizontal slab bearing the insignia of the 3rd Division, two other monuments salute the unit's artillery and one of its regiments, the South Lancashire, which liberated the village. During the summer months, the tourist information bureau displays an exhibition of photographs and various objects including a scale model of the Sword Beach Gooseberry. A Centaur tank is on display not far from there, towards Colleville. Right next to it, facing the sea, a monument salutes the decisive role played by the seamen in the success of the invasion.

The division's HQ and a field hospital were set up in the castle grounds (now the town hall), in the centre of the village, some small way inland. Two plaques, one on either side of the entrance gate, remind us of this. Across the road, a small stele pays tribute to Harold Pickersgill, "Honorary citizen of the village". Pickersgill was one of those who secretly worked in Britain on the drawing of a map, based on information gleaned from aerial photographs and the Resistance, for the purposes of the invasion. In 1944, he obtained permission to land at Hermanville, a sector he knew well, as he had mapped it. He married a French woman after the war and settled in Normandy, where he died in 1998. On the little square near the church, the visitor will find a strange object. For having supplied the troops with the water they needed, a plaque informs us that the Mare Saint-Pierre well has the honour of having been included on the roll of the British army. From this square, a small path leads to the military cemetery and its 1,005 graves, for the most part those of British soldiers killed during the landing at Sword Beach or during the 3rd Division's advance towards Caen. ∎

• Monument paying tribute to the 150,000 seamen who took part in the landings •

• The Mare Saint-Pierre well •

COLLEVILLE / MONTGOMERY

Lieutenant Commander Kieffer's French marines and their British comrades of N°4 Commando landed on Colleville Beach, at the western extremity of Queen Red. At the edge of the beach, a bas-relief sculpture symbolically facing an impressive blockhouse is dedicated to their memory.

A granite stele, also dedicated to their memory, indicates the beginning of the Avenue du 4ème Commando, situated at the meeting point of Colleville and Ouistreham beaches. Opposite it stands one of the oldest monuments

• Bas-relief paying tribute to the Commandos •

• One of the bunkers on the Hillman site •

commemorating the landings. It was erected on 6th June 1944 on the spot where the first Allied soldiers to die during the assault were provisionally buried and pays homage to the men of Kieffer's commando unit and to the British troops. A special mention is dedicated to their commander, General Montgomery, whose name has been joined to that of the village, as requested by the town council as a pledge of gratitude. Crossing the coast road, the visitor will discover a very lifelike statue of the famous "Monty", unveiled by the Duke of Kent in 1996 in the middle of a small square.

The village of Colleville, situated a little over a mile inland, was flanked by several fortified positions. Just west of the village, the WN 16 (code-named Morris by the British) housed a battery of four 100-mm guns. The battery had a Polish gun crew who put up little resistance, and it fell around 1300 hours. The same could not be said of WN 17 (code-named Hillman), situated south west of the village, whose difficult capture delayed the British advance on Caen. This vast entrenchment, where the HQ of the 736th Infantry Regiment was established, was equipped with powerful defensive weapons (anti-tank guns, machine guns etc.) surrounding a series of blockhouses. It stubbornly resisted the men of the 1st Suffolk, supported by tanks, who were charged with capturing it. Hillman only fell late in the evening, after ten hours of fighting. For some years now, the initiatives of a volunteer organisation has made it possible to restore the site and to open it to visitors. ∎

• Field Marshal Bernard L. Montgomery •

• Stele to the memory of the first Allied soldiers to fall on 6th June 1944 •

OUISTREHAM

• "The Flame" monument. On the left is Lieutenant Commander Kieffer's stele.
The stones in the foreground bear the names of the French commandos killed on the beach •

The peaceful seaside resort of Ouistreham-Riva-Bella, controlling the Orne estuary and the entrance to the canal, had been turned into a *Stützpunkt* (fortified position) by the Germans. The majority of the seafront villas had been knocked down to make way for a veritable entrenched camp, bristling with bunkers, armoured shelters, guns, machine gun nests and mortars.

One of the most powerful batteries on the Lower Normandy coast was established here on the beach itself. It was equipped with six 155-mm guns set in concrete

• One of the 155-mm guns in place on Riva Bella beach •

• Remains of "dragon's teeth" anti-tank defences •

vats. Nevertheless, lacking pillboxes to protect them from airborne attacks, the guns had been transferred inland shortly before the landings. Whereas not a trace of the battery remains, nor of the many anti-tank positions that covered the site, there are several remains of smaller defensive constructions behind the cabins lining the beach.

Finally, the imposing firing command post, nearly 60 feet high, has escaped demolition. It now houses the Atlantic Wall Museum.

To complete the system, another battery was constructed south of the village, near the water tower. Its bunkers are still in existence, but access to them is not easy. The men of N°4 Commando, who landed at Colleville just after 0730, had the difficult task of

• A "Tobruk" shelter •

capturing Ouistreham. Lieutenant commander Philippe Kieffer's 177 marines, the only Frenchmen active on the ground on D-Day, spear-headed this deployment. When they regrouped in the ruins of a holiday camp, they had already lost 40 of their comrades, dead or wounded, on the beach.

Their losses were no less severe as they advanced through Ouistreham, capturing fortified positions one by one, under sniper fire. While the British

were vigorously battling their way to conquering the battery on the beach, the Frenchmen reached the area round the Casino. Although no offence is intended to Daryl Zanuck, the building looked nothing like its depiction in the film "The Longest Day" in 1944... because it had been demolished in 1943 to clear the firing area. Only the foundations had been conserved, and the building transformed into a fortification. Tank support was needed before the position fell around 0930 hours.

The firing command post remained in German hands in rather unusual conditions. Having repelled a first assault, which had not been followed up, its occupants were careful not to show themselves, and in the hope of being forgotten. It was not until 10th June that, by chance, a British patrol tumbled to their ploy on attempting to enter the large bunker and obtained the surrender of the 53-man garrison without difficulty.

Obviously, Kieffer's commandos are highly honoured in Ouistreham today. The stele dedicated to their leader, near the "The Flame" monument (symbol of the French Resistance), symbolically erected on a former armoured machine gun shelter, is complemented by a plaque affixed to the Landings Committee signal monument, situated on the roundabout at the entrance to the town, not forgetting the N°4 Commando museum. ■

• Monument paying
tribute to
the Royal Navy
crews and Commandos •

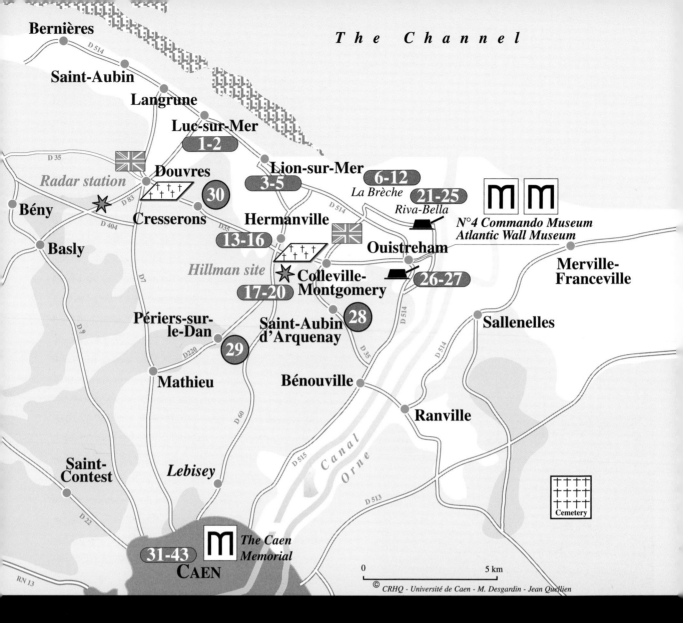

The Channel

Bernières
Saint-Aubin
Langrune
Luc-sur-Mer
1-2
Lion-sur-Mer
3-5
6-12
La Brèche
21-25
Riva-Bella
M M
N°4 Commando Museum
Atlantic Wall Museum
D 35
Radar station
Douvres
30
Bény
Cresserons
Hermanville
Ouistreham
Merville-Franceville
Basly
13-16
Hillman site
Colleville-
Montgomery
26-27
17-20
Sallenelles
28
Périers-sur-le-Dan
Saint-Aubin
d'Arquenay
29
Mathieu
Bénouville
Ranville
Canal
Orne
Saint-Contest
Lebisey
Cemetery
M
The Caen Memorial
31-43
CAEN
0   5 km
© *CRHQ - Université de Caen - M. Desgardin - Jean Quellien*

LUC-SUR-MER
1. Monument to the Allied raid in September 1941 and the liberation of the town
2. Monument to General Leclerc and the 2nd Armoured Division (Route de Douvres)

LION-SUR-MER
3. Monument to N° 41 Commando
4. Monument to the 77th Armoured Engineer Squadron
5. Stele - 40th Anniversary of the liberation of Lion-sur-Mer

HERMANVILLE "LA BRÈCHE"
6. Stele - South Lancashire
7. Monument to the 3rd Division Royal Artillery
8. Liberation monument
9. D-Day stained glass window "La Brèche" (chapel)
10. Admiral Wietzel memorial (Boulevard de la 3ème Division)
11. Monument to Allied seamen
12. Plaque to the memory of the staff officers of the 9th Brigade (Rue du Clos Moulin)

HERMANVILLE BOURG
13. Plaque - Mare Saint-Pierre well
14. Plaque - 3rd Division HQ (town hall)

15. Plaque - Field hospital (town hall)
16. Stele - Harold Pickersgill (village hall)

COLLEVILLE-MONTGOMERY
17. Statue of General Montgomery
18. N° 4 Commando monument
19. Provisional cemetery monument
20. Plaque - Suffolk Regiment (Hillman site)

OUISTREHAM RIVA-BELLA
21. "La Flamme" monument
22. Stele - Lieutenant commander Kieffer
23. Monument to the Royal Navy seamen and Royal Marines (port)
24. Plaques - N° 4 Commando and tribute to Captain Lion (Rue Pasteur)
25. Stele to the memory of Commandos Hubert, Labas, Lemoigne & Letang (Boulevard Churchill)

OUISTREHAM BOURG
26. Commandos and Scottish 51st Division stained glass window (church)
27. Landing Committee signal Monument and N° 4 Commando plaque

SAINT-AUBIN-D'ARQUENAY
28. Monument to the commandos of the 1st Special Service Brigade

PÉRIERS-SUR-LE-DAN
29. Stele - 3rd Infantry Division

CRESSERONS
30. Stele - 22nd Dragoons

CAEN
31. Stele - 50th anniversary of the liberation by the Canadians
32. Stele - Canadian soldiers who fell for the liberation of Caen
33. Monument to the Stormont, Dundas and Glengarry Highlanders
34. Monument to the British 3rd Division
35. Plaque - memorial to those shot on 6th June
36. Monument to those shot on 6th June
37. Monument to the people of Caen who were deported or shot
38. Stele - Patriotic ceremony on 9th July 1944
39. Civilian victims' square and monument
40. Monument to Caen's ordeal
41. Plaque - Refugees in Saint-Étienne church
42. Plaque - Emergency teams
43. Stele - General de Gaulle

LION-SUR-MER

• N°41 Royal Marine Commando Monument •

The shore at Lion-sur-Mer and Luc-sur-Mer being maladapted to landing operations, both these seaside resorts had to be captured by means of assaults launched from Hermanville to the east and Langrune to the west. N°41 Commando experienced the greatest of difficulties in dislodging the Germans from Lion, in spite of support from tanks and supporting fire from the navy. During the evening of the 7th, however, following the capture of the last enemy positions, the Royal Marines linked up with N°s 46 and 48 Commando in Luc-sur-Mer, thus giving the British control of the whole coastal sector from Port-en-Bessin to Ouistreham. The previous day, taking advantage of the delayed linking up with the Canadians, a detachment of tanks from the 21st Panzer had succeeded in infiltrating the lines and reaching the beach between Lion and Luc around 8 o'clock in the evening. Finding themselves isolated, this unit decided to retreat without having turned the situation to their advantage. The spectacular monument to N°41 Commando erected on the Route de Luc takes the unusual form of a sundial. At the foot of the edifice, a plaque recalls the sequence of events on 6th June including an extract from a speech by President Roosevelt evoking the fundamental liberties that had to be protected from dictatorships. ■

LUC-SUR-MER

• The monument at Luc-sur-Mer •

"Passer-by, stand and reflect" can be read on the stele standing on the seafront promenade. Two events are evoked there. First of all, the raid during the night of 28th September 1941 by a small Allied commando unit on reconnaissance. The second recalls the liberation of the village on 7th June by Royal Marines of N°46 Commando, who had landed that same morning at Saint-Aubin, after the fierce fighting to capture a small group of houses the Germans had fortified at the hamlet called "Le Petit Enfer" ("Little Hell"). After the liberation of Luc, the Hotel Belle Plage (since transformed into seafront housing), requisitioned by the British, became a place of rest and relaxation for the men of the 3rd Infantry Division during the Battle of Normandy. ■

Close-up

ON THE DOUVRES RADAR STATION

• 50-mm gun •

The 50-mm anti-tank gun defending the Douvres radar station.

• "Wasserman" radar •

The "Wasserman" radar antenna (destroyed by aerial bombardment before the landings) measured over 120 feet in height.

• "*Würzburg*" radar •

The "*Würzburg*" radar reinstalled on the site at Douvres in 1994.

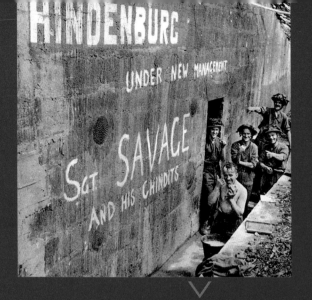

• The "Hindenburg" bunker •

Sergeant Savage and his men of the 102nd Anti-aircraft Artillery Regiment captured the "Hindenburg" bunker.

• The "Anton" bunker

A corridor inside the "Anton" bunker. The radio room is at the far end.

• The "Anton" bunker •

Reconstitution of a room reserved for the garrison's barracks.

In 1942, the Germans built a large Lüftwaffe radar detection station west of the village of Douvres on a plateau about 3 miles from the shore, which was code-named "Distelfink" (Goldfinch). It covered nearly 25 acres and was composed of two installations, one on each side of the road to Bény. The northern part was equipped with a "Wasserman" radar, used for long-range spotting of the surrounding airspace. The southern part, which was larger, included two medium-range Freya radar and two parabolic Würzburg-Reise dishes ; the whole station was completed by many partially buried concrete buildings, for use by the garrison or as munitions stores and a large bunker with twenty-odd rooms housing the operations room and command post. It was solidly fortified, and constituted a veritable entrenched camp, surrounded by minefields, barbed wire and trenches, defended by anti-tank guns and machine gun nests.

During the decisive hours, the Douvres radar station was to prove incapable of fulfilling the task for which it had been built, as it had been copiously bombarded before the invasion, as had all the stations in the Seine Bay and on the North Sea coast and, like them, was moreover subjected to intense jamming during the night of 5th - 6th June. Its defensive system was, nevertheless, still intact.

So the Canadian and British troops decided to skirt the obstacle and move on Caen without wasting any time. The "Distelfink" position, defended by 230 men, was thus to remain isolated behind Allied lines and held out for twelve days against the commandos who were trying to overrun it. It finally surrendered on 17th June following a by-the-book offensive led by the special tanks of the 79th Armoured Division.

As part of the D-Day 50th Anniversary celebrations, part of the Douvres radar station site was renovated, including the opening of a museum in the main bunker ("Anton"). A Würzburg-Reise telescope, identical to the ones with which "Distelfink" was equipped in 1944 and retrieved from the observatory in Paris, has been installed on site. ■

CAEN

• The devastated city of Caen a few months after its liberation •

Caen, the main town in the Calvados department, and the largest town in Lower Normandy, had a population of 60,000 in 1944, and was to suffer particularly brutally from the conflict that summer. When the fighting was done, three quarters of the "anvil on which victory was wrought", in the words of the British historian Alexander McKee, had been destroyed and the city was mourning 2,000 civilian dead.

In the Allies' plans, Caen should have been captured on the evening of 6th June but, because they had been held up as they moved south from the coast, neither the Canadians nor the British managed to achieve their objective. Over the following days, the Germans established a solid defensive barrier in front of the town, with support from several armoured divisions, including the formidable 12th Panzer SS "Hitlerjugend". After a terrible siege, the town had to wait until 9th July for its left bank to be liberated, and ten days longer for the right bank to follow suite.

Meanwhile, Caen had suffered incessant artillery fire and a series of lethal aerial bombardments. The first of these, on 6th June around 1330 hours, was aimed at the bridges over the Orne. It was badly targeted and destroyed the town centre between the castle and the river, costing the lives of 600 people. That night, it had become a

• A Canadian patrol in the Rue Saint-Pierre •

• Saint-Étienne church and the Abbaye-aux-Hommes (now the town hall), which was home to the Lycée Malherbe in 1944, provided shelter for thousands of refugees during the siege of Caen •

question of deliberately destroying the town to prevent German armoured reinforcements from driving through it. The last major bombardment, on 7th July, north of the town, heralded the final Anglo-Canadian assault. From 6th June onwards, a large part of the population left Caen, some in a massive southward exodus, others to hide in the underground quarries such as those at Fleury-sur-Orne. But between 10,000 and 15,000 people stayed put, most of them seeking refuge in the western part of the town, spared from the bombs under the roof of Saint-Étienne church, the various buildings of the Abbaye-aux-Hommes or the annexes of the Bon Sauveur psychiatric hospital.

Many monuments pay tribute to the liberators, the 3rd Canadian Division and the British 3rd Division. Others have been erected to the memory of the civilian victims. Finally, tribute is also paid to the Resistance, particularly the 70 or 80 misfortunate prisoners summarily executed by the Gestapo on the morning of 6th June. ■

• Refugees in Saint-Étienne church •

AD PERPETUAM MEMORIAM   EN PERPETUELLE MEMOIRE

ANNO DNI MCMXLIV FIDE MUNITI ET EXEMPLO
RR. DD. LEONIS GOURDIER DES HAMEAUX
PAROCHI HUJUS ECCLESIAE ROBORATI
CIVES CADOMENSES INSTANTE PUGNA PRO
LIBERTATE IN HAC ORATIONIS DOMO VITAM
ET SPEM SUAM IN TUTO COMMISERUNT

L'AN 1944, PENDANT LA BATAILLE LIBÉRATRICE,
LES CAENNAIS, SOUTENUS PAR LEUR FOI ET
L'EXEMPLE DU CURÉ-DOYEN DE SAINT-ÉTIENNE,
LÉON GOURDIER DES HAMEAUX, ONT ABRITÉ
LEUR VIE ET LEUR ESPÉRANCE SOUS LES
VOÛTES DE CETTE ÉGLISE

• Plaque – "In perpetual memory" •

• Refugees crowded into Saint-Étienne church, part of the Abbaye-aux-Hommes •

• Caen at a glance •

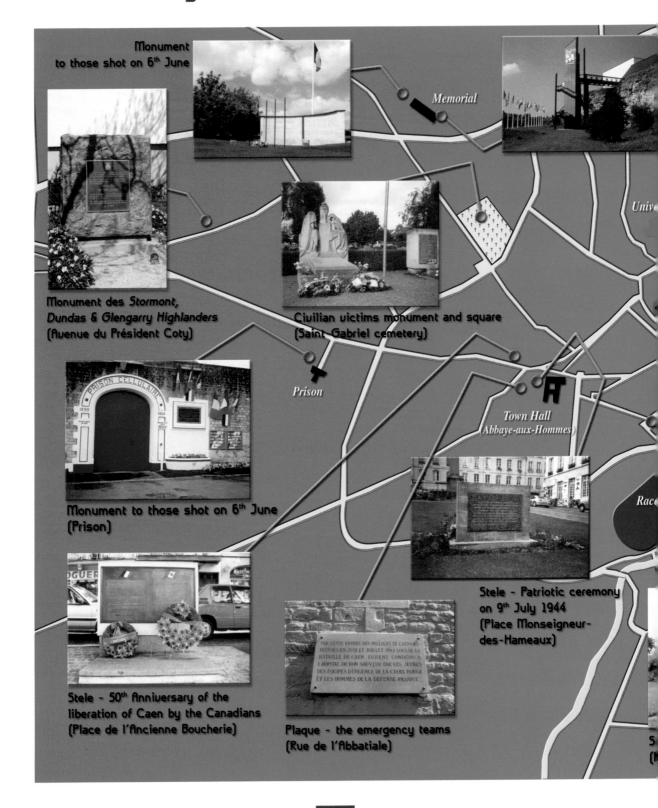

Monument
to those shot on 6th June

Memorial

Monument des *Stormont,
Dundas & Glengarry Highlanders*
(Avenue du Président Coty)

Civilian victims monument and square
(Saint-Gabriel cemetery)

Univ

Prison

Town Hall
(Abbaye-aux-Hommes)

Race

Monument to those shot on 6th June
(Prison)

Stele - Patriotic ceremony
on 9th July 1944
(Place Monseigneur-
des-Hameaux)

Stele - 50th Anniversary of the
liberation of Caen by the Canadians
(Place de l'Ancienne Boucherie)

Plaque - the emergency teams
(Rue de l'Abbatiale)

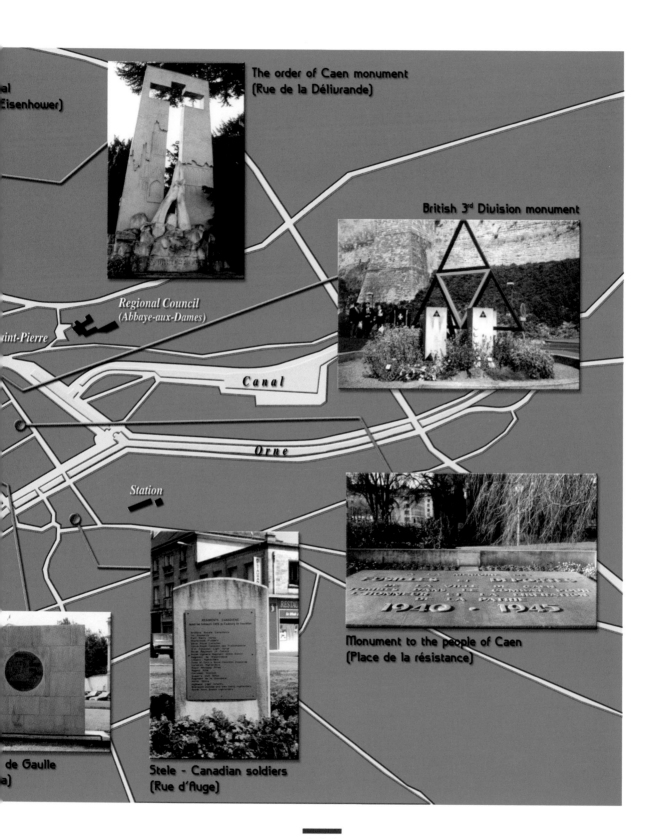

al
(Eisenhower)

The order of Caen monument
(Rue de la Délivrande)

British 3rd Division monument

Regional Council
(Abbaye-aux-Dames)

int-Pierre

Canal

Orne

Station

Monument to the people of Caen
(Place de la résistance)

de Gaulle
a)

Stele - Canadian soldiers
(Rue d'Auge)

• The patriotic ceremony behind Saint-Étienne church on 9th July at the end of the afternoon, in the presence of the Allies and the Fred Scaramoni FFI •

• Caen - Place Monseigneur-des-Hameaux •

• The Canadians entering Caen on 9th July after over a month of siege •

m for useums

Musée DU N°4 COMMANDO

OUISTREHAM

Situated near the casino, the N°4 Commando museum retraces the history of this elite unit, which landed on Sword Beach on the morning of 6th June with the particularly dangerous mission of capturing the very heavily defended town of Ouistreham, by means of objects, symbolic documents and models.

N°4 Commando, under the command of Colonel Dawson, consisted of 8 units, six British and two French belonging to the 1st Battalion of marines, a commando unit commanded by Lieutenant-commander Philippe Kieffer.

Musée DU MUR DE L'ATLANTIQUE

OUISTREHAM

The impressive firing command post of Ouistreham battery, over 55 feet high and comprising 5 levels, now houses the Atlantic Wall museum.

Every level has been carefully reconstructed, using devices, weapons, objects, mannequins etc. In the upper part, a powerful telemeter with a range of 25 miles covered the Seine Bay. Another room tells the story of the construction of the Atlantic Wall, that gigantic undertaking that mobilised hundreds of thousands of workers and caused millions of tonnes of concrete to be poured.

Musée LE MÉMORIAL DE CAEN

© P. Canino

The Caen Memorial, inaugurated on 6th June 1988, opened its new spaces to the public in March 2002. The historical voyage consecrated to the Second World War, D-Day, and the Battle of Normandy has been enriched with new spaces: the World and the Cold War, and Worlds for Peace.

The Memorial is a very modern museum with a wealth different photos, films, maps, arrangements of objects from daily and military life, audio eye-witness accounts, archives, works of art, interactive terminals and hands-on exhibits and games. Amongst the main objects on display are a Soviet MIG-21, an American H-Bomb, the remains of the American U2 spy plane shot down over Cuba, two section of the Berlin Wall and a monumental facsimile of the first ever Peace treaty in humanity's history. The films "0" and "The Battle of Normandy", digital projections on giant screens, and "Nuclear Terror" on a circular screen are not to be missed.

© P. Canino

Bénouville - Pégasus Bridge

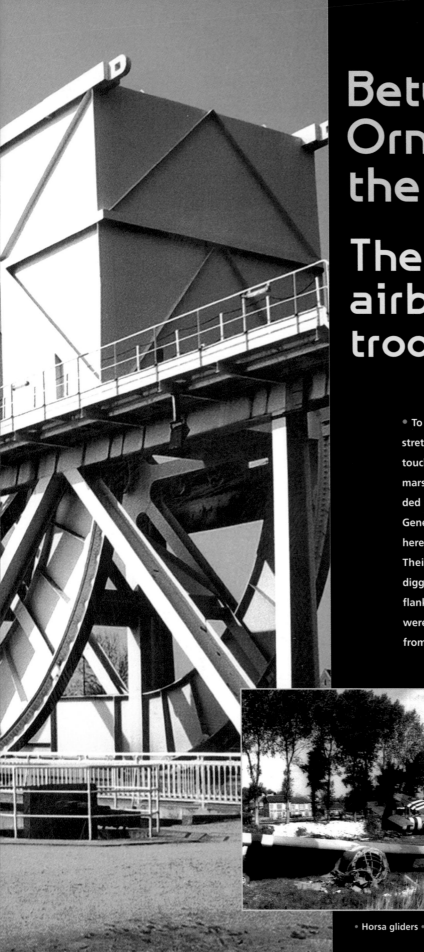

Between the Orne and the Dives,

The British airborne troops' sector

● To the east of the Orne estuary stretches an area of low-lying country touching the Caen plain and the Dives marshland, which was voluntarily flooded by the Germans in 1944. The men of General Gale's 6th Airborne were to drop here during the night of 5th to 6th June. Their essential mission consisted in digging into this zone to protect the left flank of the sector, from which the Allies were to launch their daybreak assault, from German counter-offensives.

›

● Horsa gliders ●

• The day before the offensive, General Gale talking to the men of the 6th Airborne •

Some groups were given precise objectives. For example, a series of bridges over the Dives and its tributary the Divette, at Troarn, Bures, Robehomme and Varaville had to be destroyed to prevent the rapid intervention of the units of the German 15th Army in position to the east of the river. On the other hand, the two interconnecting bridges at Ranville and Bénouville crossing the Orne and the canal had to be captured intact. They were the only means of crossing from one bank to the other between Caen and the sea, and would enable the troops coming from Sword Beach to bring their support rapidly to the airborne troops. This delicate mission was entrusted to the 2nd Battalion *Ox and Bucks* (Oxford and Buckinghamshire Light Infantry) under Major Howard, who crossed the Channel in six gliders. Simultaneously, a

parachute battalion was to capture the battery at Merville, whose four supposedly 150-mm guns it was feared would cause serious damage on the nearest landing beaches.

In spite of all these difficulties, and frequently demonstrating valiant courage the "Red Berets" achieved all the tasks that had been assigned to them. Meanwhile, the main part of the 6th Airborne landed on Norman soil shortly before one in the morning, not without some losses. Many men became lost, some even falling straight into the marshes. Around half past three at first wave of gliders brought fresh troops and heavy weaponry. Another followed at the end of the day. A defensive perimeter was set up around the bridges of Ranville and Bénouville to contain the first German counter-

• "The Channel stopped you, but not us..." •

offensives and the first reinforcements reached there in the early afternoon, thus closing the gap between the troops landing on Sword Beach and the 6th Airborne. Violent fighting for possession of the ridge running from Sallenelles to Troarn took place over the following days, notably around Amfréville and Bréville. Then the front settled down and a long and exhausting war of position began, a war of patrols and raids under artillery bombardment and mortar fire.

Operation Paddle was to be launched from this narrow bridgehead to the east of the Orne in mid-August, at the same time as the Germans were being surrounded in the Falaise pocket. The offensive drive to the Seine was launched by a very cosmopolitan army including British and Canadian troops, the Belgian Piron Brigade, the Dutch Princess Irene Brigade, and the Frenchmen of Kieffer's unit. ∎

• Paratroops in defensive position at a cross-roads near Ranville •

• German fortifications near the Baie de Sallenelles •

Bénouville

• Pegasus Bridge in British hands. Horsa gliders in the background, just a few yards from the bridge •

On 6th June at 0015 hours the three Horsa gliders carrying Major Howard's men achieved the feat of landing just a few yards from the bridge at Bénouville. Small stone blocks on the small path that runs along the canal mark the exact spot where each glider drew to a halt. A bronze bust of Major Howard

has been erected near the first of these.

The element of surprise had its full effect and the raiders managed to capture the bridge, hardly firing a shot. With reinforcements from the paratroops, they were to have to hold on to the position and repel German counter-attacks, notably from the 21st Panzer, until the arrival of the first Commando brigade at about one in the afternoon. Contrary to the legend, Bill Millin stopped playing his bagpipes, so as not to draw unwanted enemy fire, when he crossed the bridge with Lord Lovat. This first success on a day that was full of them has secured world renown for the modest village of Bénouville and its bridge, the now legendary Pegasus Bridge.

• Bust of Major Howard •

On the Major John Howard Esplanade, beside the Landings Committee signal monument, there is a plaque dedicated to the "*Ox and Bucks*" and the German anti-tank gun whose mission was defending the bridge. On the opposite bank, the famous Gondrée café,

• The legendary Gondrée café
"the first French house to be liberated" •

the "first house in France to be liberated in the last hour of 5th June" as a plaque affixed to its façade proudly states, has become a favourite rendezvous for the veterans of the 6th Airborne every D-Day anniversary. For its part, the town hall prides itself in being the first in France to have been liberated... on 5th June at 2345 hours. Sceptical observers are reminded that differences between French time and British time (two, between the old and the new) not forgetting German time that had been imposed at the beginning of the occupation complicate the equation... and make it easier to try and go one better.

Bénouville and Ranville bridges being unable to cope with all the traffic between the two banks, the British engineers launched the construction of several metal bridges both upstream and down. They were dismantled in the autumn to be used elsewhere. Around 400 yards from the Gondrée café towards Caen along the canal-side path, a stele recalls the existence of one of these structures called "London Bridge", which was the first Bailey bridge to be built in France, three days after the invasion. A Bailey bridge, found in a shed, is now presented on the spot.

Following disagreements between the Gondrée family, owners of the land, and the Landings Committee, which ran the establishment, the museum opened in 1974 not far from the café closed its doors in 1997. The Pegasus memorial, which opened in June 2000, took up where its predecessor left off. It lies between the canal and the Orne and its historic space encompasses the venerable Bénouville Bridge, which was dismantled in 1993 due to new navigational requirements on the canal and replaced with a much larger "twin brother".

In summer, a high quality son et lumière show is put on in the place where the great D-Day adventure began. ■

• Stele recalling the first Bailey bridge to be built across the canal to reduce the bottleneck at Pegasus Bridge •

RANVILLE

• A few dozen yards now separate the new Bénouville Bridge from its venerable predecessor, Pegasus Bridge, that is now housed in the Ranville museum •

While Major Howard's men were busy capturing Bénouville Bridge a few hundred yards away, Lieutenant Fox and his troop captured the swing bridge over the Orne at Ranville without difficulty, its guards losing no time in taking to their heels. "Horsa Bridge" never achieved the prestige that its neighbour did. Nevertheless, a stele indicates the conditions in which it was captured by the men of the two gliders that managed to set down nearby, a third having become lost nearly twenty miles away.

The paratroops of the 5th Brigade captured the village that can thus, and rightfully, pride itself on being the "first village in France to be liberated". A plaque on the wall of a broad field, where the gliders carrying the heavy weaponry landed a short while later, indicates that it was by then 0230. We will not make any more of that here, given the problem of the time differences already mentioned. In any case, General Gale established his HQ in Ranville during the night. Gale was commander of the 6th Airborne and a bronze bust in his likeness now stands near the town hall, at the entrance to the municipal library.

Most of the paratroops who fell victim to the fighting on 6th June and the following weeks were buried in the Ranville military cemetery, alongside a few hundred German soldiers. There are, however, some graves in the village cemetery right beside it. There lies Lieutenant "Den" Brotheridge, fatally wounded as he led his men in the charge on the bridge at Bénouville. He was without doubt the first Allied soldier killed in the fighting in Normandy. On the Place Général Gale, on a low wall opposite the entrance to the military cemetery, a series of panels explains the operations undertaken by the 6th Airborne on the 6th June. Not far from there, a plaque on the side of a former mill recalls the participation of the Belgian soldiers in the final part of the Battle of Normandy. The brigade commanded by Colonel Jean Piron, which became part of the British 2nd Army, joined the fighting in the middle of the month of August and shared in the liberation of the Calvados coast

from Cabourg to Honfleur. At the foot of the old mill, the town of Ranville has erected a memorial paying tribute to Major Stafford, who devoted his whole life to ensuring the perpetuation of the memory of his comrades' sacrifice. ■

• The grave of Lieutenant Brotheridge, the first Allied soldier to be killed in Normandy •

• Bust of General Gale, commander of the 6th Airborne •

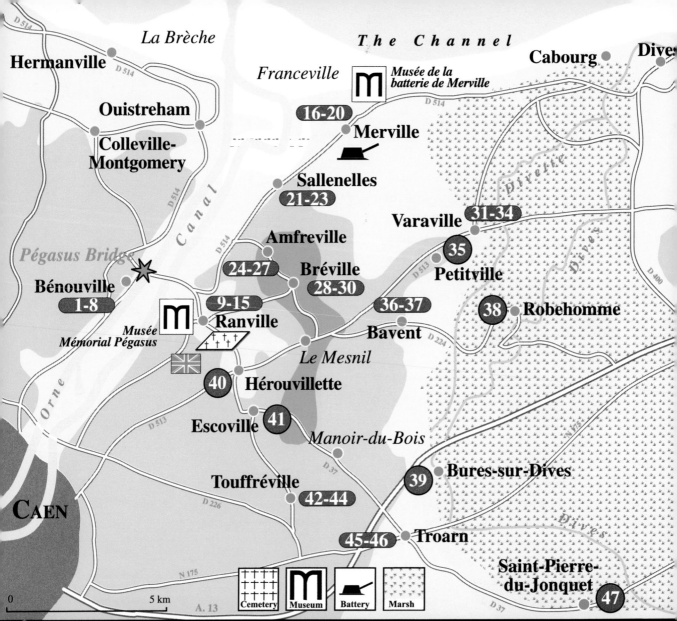

© CRHQ - Université de Caen - M. Desgardin - Jean Quellien

- **BÉNOUVILLE**
1. Bust of Major Howard
2. Stones marking the places the gliders landed
3. Plaque - 2nd Battalion *Ox & Bucks*
4. Landings Committee signal monument
5. Plaque - first house liberated (Café Gondrée)
6. Plaque - first town hall liberated
7. Monument to the 7th Parachute Battalion
8. Stele - first Bailey bridge built in France
- **RANVILLE**
9. Stele - Horsa Bridge
10. Plaque - first village liberated in France
11. Plaque - Lieutenant Brotheridge (village cemetery)
12. Wall with plaques recounting operations on 6th June
13. Major Stafford memorial
14. Plaque - Belgian fighters of the Piron Brigade
15. Bust of General Gale
- **MERVILLE-FRANCEVILLE**
16. Memorial to the 9th Parachute Battalion
17. Bust of Lieutenant-colonel Otway
18. Monument to N°45 Commando
19. Monument to the Belgian soldiers (Piron Brigade) killed on 18th August 1944
20. Memorial to the liberators and civilian victims

- **SALLENELLES**
21. Monument to the 4th Special Service Brigade
22. Plaque - first Belgian soldier killed in France
23. Monument to the Belgian soldiers in the Piron Brigade
- **AMFRÉVILLE**
24. Monument to N° 3 Commando
25. Monument to N° 4 Commando
26. Stele - N° 6 Commando
27. Monument to the 1st Special Service Brigade
- **BRÉVILLE**
28. Stele - 12th Parachute Battalion
29. Stele - Battle of Bois-des-Monts (Saint-Côme Castle)
30. Stele - Captain Ward and Private Masters
- **VARAVILLE**
31. Memorial to the 1st Canadian Parachute battalion
32. Stele - N° 3 Commando
33. Stele - 3rd Parachute Squadron of the Royal Engineers
34. Stele - Piron Brigade
- **PETITVILLE**
35. Stele - N° 3 Commando
- **BAVENT**
36. Monument to the 3rd Parachute Brigade (Le Mesnil)

- **ROBEHOMME**
38. Plaque - Canadian 1st Parachute Battalion (Presbytery)
- **BURES**
39. Stele - 3rd Parachute Squadron of the Royal Engineers
- **HÉROUVILLETTE**
Plaque - 2nd Battalion *Ox & Bucks*
- **ESCOVILLE**
41. Stele - 2nd Battalion *Ox & Bucks*
- **TOUFFRÉVILLE**
42. Stele - 8th Battalion of the Parachute Regiment (Manoir du Bois)
43. Stele - Brigadier Pearson (Manoir du Bois)
44. Stele - Privates Platt and Billington, executed by the Nazis
- **TROARN**
45. Stele - Major Roseveare (Saint-Samson Bridge)
46. Plaque - 3rd Parachute Squadron of the Royal Engineers
- **SAINT-PIERRE-DU-JONQUET**
47. Monument to those shot

MERVILLE - FRANCEVILLE

• The Merville battery bunker •

• Bust of Lieutenant-colonel Otway •

The Germans had installed a series of secondary defensive positions east of the Orne estuary. Many remains of these fortifications are still to be found on the beach and in the Varaville dunes, near an old 18th Century fort. The artillery in this sector, 47 or 50-mm, hardly posed a threat to the troops who were going to attack on the other side of the river, because of their insufficient range.

On the other hand, the battery situated south of the small town of Merville, further inland, with its four bunkers housing – according to the British intelligence report – 150-mm guns, constituted a genuine menace that the aerial bombardments could not be sure of annihilating. Consequently, it was decided to capture it the night before the invasion. Lieutenant-colonel Otway's 9th Parachute Battalion trained intensely for the mission to capture this fortified position, surrounded by minefields and barbed wire and defended by a garrison of nearly 150 gunners, but nothing went as planned.

Due to the very wide-ranging dispersal of his men during the drop, Otway only managed to assemble

150 or so, deprived of most of their material, instead of the 600 originally making up his unit. Moreover, the three gliders that were to have landed inside the defensive perimeter were nowhere to be seen. Nevertheless, they launched the assault. And yet, after a furious battle, which resulted in heavy losses in the ranks of the attackers and left very few survivors on the German side, their objective was attained. The battery was in British hands shortly before 0500 hours. The successful assailants were surprised to discover that the guns were less powerful than had been thought. Specialists are still discussing their size. Were they 75-mm bore or 100-mm ? Whatever the case, they were not a major threat to Sword Beach.

This does not diminish the fact that the capture of the Merville battery constitutes one of D-Day's great feats of arms. A museum established in a former bunker tells the story of this heroic deed. At the entrance to the site, a stele has been erected in tribute to the 9th Parachute Battalion. A bronze bust immortalises the determination of its commander, Lieutenant-colonel Otway. ■

A MFRÉVILLE

• Amfréville, June 1944. The French marines of N°4 Commando back with their compatriots •

The village of Amfréville, liberated on the evening of 6th June, became the meeting place and the HQ of the various units constituting Lord Lovat's 1st Special Service Brigade, including Lt. Commander Kieffer's French marines. These units defended the north of the bridgehead against German attacks to the east of the Orne. Alongside the paratroops, during the days following D-Day, the commandos notably repelled powerful offensives launched by the 346th Division, which had been stationed in Rouen.

• The monument to N°6 Commando, erected in front of the "Commandos' farm" •

Commemorative monuments are particularly numerous here. At the entrance to the village of Amfréville - Le Plain, in front of the "Commandos' Farm", a stele pays special tribute to N°6 Commando. Further on, in front of the church, on the Place du Commandant Kieffer, a very early monument, inaugurated in July 1944, is dedicated "to the memory of the officers and men of the 1st Special Brigade who lost their lives in the fight for Normandy". Erected around the same time, the little monument to N°4 Commando is located on the Place du Colonel Dawson (commander of the unit) on the hillock at Oger (or Hauger) hamlet at the edge of the village on the way to Sallenelles. The stele to N°3 Commando, which dates from the 55th anniversary of the invasion, has been erected near the town hall. ∎

• Monument to N°4 Commando.
Erected in July 1944, in the midst of battle and with whatever lay at hand (it was moulded in a washing basin), this small monument is the oldest of all those commemorating the events of summer 1944. It is conceived in the Scottish tradition, a cairn made with as many stones as there were men in the Commando unit ; 177 of them symbolise Lieutenant commander Keiffer's French combatants •

B RÉVILLE

• Stele - Battle of Bois-des-Monts, near Saint-Côme castle •

The Germans had established strongholds on the Bréville heights, positions that dominated and threatened the British. They had, therefore, to be captured. The village, which was taken by the commandos on 7th June and devastated by the bombardments, was lost to a counter-offensive. On 11th June, reinforcements in the form of the Black Watch Regiment of the Scottish 51st Division, which had just arrived on the bridgehead, were given a severe thrashing and had to retreat. A renewed assault on the evening of 12th June launched by the paratroops finally succeeded in dislodging the Germans, with heavy losses on both sides. Bréville was in British hands, but the castle of Saint-Côme, perched on a neighbouring hill, was to remain a no-man's land that both camps wrestled over until August. The memorial erected at Bréville crossroads pays tribute to the men who captured the village and notably to the 162 airborne troops killed during the clash, including Colonel Johnson, the commander of the 12th parachute Battalion. Near Saint-Côme castle another monument paying tribute to the 9th Parachute Battalion recalls the fighting in that sector, now referred to as the Battle of Bois-des-Monts. ∎

TROARN

• The team with which Major Roseveare managed to destroy the bridge at Saint-Samson must have looked very like this one •

Over three-quarters of the little market town of Troarn was destroyed by the fighting there before it was liberated on 17th August. In the very first hours of 6th June, it had been the scene of a particularly spectacular event. The destruction of the Saint-Samson bridge, at the edge of the village on the road to Dozulé, was part of the mission assigned to the 3rd Parachute Squadron of the Royal Engineers, who dropped... 6 miles away, near Ranville. Its commander, Major Roseveare, sending the rest of his men on foot in the direction of the other bridges over the Dives, took charge of the operation personally. Piled onto a jeep towing a trailer full of explosives, with nine sappers and an officer, they set off for Troarn. At the entrance to the village, a guard was imprudently killed by a with a burst from a machine gun, with the result that the whole garrison came out into the main street. Roseveare and his heavy material ran a hellish gauntlet of fire through Troarn, accelerator to the floor, losing one of their number, who was thrown from the vehicle, on the way. The descent to the Dives enabled them to gain speed and get out of range. At 0520 the bridge blew. A stele recalls Major Roseveare and his men's feat. For his part, Captain Juckes managed to destroy the two bridges at Bures in the same manner around 0930 hours. A memorial pays tribute to this young officer who was killed in fighting some weeks later. ■

SAINT-PIERRE-DU-JONQUET

The monument in Saint-Pierre-du-Jonquet pays tribute to the 28 local inhabitants who were savagely executed by the Nazis during the Battle of Normandy. Most of them were arrested for having helped the British paratroops that had become isolated following the bad drops on the night of 5th - 6th June. They were taken to Argences, to where the Caen Gestapo had retreated, and were subjected to vicious torture before being executed without trial. Their bodies, hastily thrown into bomb craters not far from there in Saint-Pierre-du-Jonquet, were discovered after the war. Eleven of them were unidentifiable. They now lie in a square in the village cemetery. It is possible that the bodies of other victims the Gestapo murdered in similar circumstances have never been found. ■

• The monument to those shot •

M for useums

Musée MÉMORIAL PÉGASUS

RANVILLE

The Pegasus Memorial Museum was inaugurated by Prince Charles in June 2000. The diverse thematic displays , with supporting film on video screens, recount the battles of the 6th Airborne and the daily life of its troops, putting the emphasis on the capture of the bridges in Bénouville and Ranville during the night of 5th - 6th June 1944.

Amongst the hundreds of personal belongings donated by the veterans and private individuals are the beret worn by Major Howard on D-Day and Bill Millin's bagpipes.

Various types of British artillery and a half-track are on display around the venerable Pegasus Bridge near the museum.

Musée DE LA BATTERIE DE MERVILLE

MERVILLE

Inaugurated at the beginning of the 1980s, the Merville Battery museum is housed in one of the battery's former bunkers. By means of a collection of objects, weapons and documents, it recounts the story of this part of the Atlantic Wall and its spectacular capture by the men of Lieutenant-colonel Otway's 9th Parachute Battalion during the night of 5th - 6th June 1944. Alongside a series of mannequins in position, there are an anti-aircraft gun similar to those used in the defence of the position, and a 75-mm gun.

Photographic Credits

Allen Jones: cover, pp.1, 7 (br), 54 (m), 57 (tr), 68 (t), 72 (b), 91 (t), 101 (t), 119 (t), 123;
Archives Départementales du Calvados: pp. 44 (b), 46 (t), 71 (t), 75 (tl & mr), 81 (b), 90 (l), 94 (b), 109 (t), 110 bm), 111 (t & br), 112 (tr), 126 (b);
Associated Press: pp. 5 (l);
Bundesarchiv: pp. 4 (r), 6, 52 (t);
Bundesarchiv/A.Chazette: pp. 93 (b), 100 (bl);
Jean Quellien collection: pp. 2 (b, e, h), 4 (l), 7 (t), 9 (tl), 14-15, 19 (t), 20 (b), 21 (tm & b), 22, 23 (m), 24 (t), 25, 26, 27 (t & b), 28 (b& & t), 30 (m & b), 31 mr & br), 38 (t), 40 (ml & br), 57 (m), 58-59, 64 (b), 65 (tl), 67 (m & tr), 70 (h), 73 (b), 74 (tr), 75 (tr, bl & br), 81 (m), 83, 84 (tr), 85 (tl), 86 (m), 87 (b), 88, 89 (b), 90 tr), 91 (m & b), 96 (t), 97 (b), 99, 100 (br), 101 (b), 103, 104 (b), 110 (tl), 112 (tl), 113 (t & m), 114, 117 (br), 118 (b), 119 (b), 121 (tr & l), 124 (b), 125, 127 (t);
J.P.Benamou collection: p. 97 (t);
Caen Memorial collection: pp. 5 (r), 9 (tr), 11 (b), 12-13, 15 (b), 21 (tl), 29, , 31 (tl, 44 (t), 96 (b), 106;
Caen Memorial collection/J.M.Piel: p. 105 (m & b);
Caen Memorial collection/F.Gendrel: p. 110 (tr);
Caen Memorial collection/M.Lechevalier: p. 44 (m);
Caen Memorial collection/R.J.Killie: p. 42 (m);
Comité du Tourisme du Calvados/DR: pp. 21 (tl), 54 (tl), 71 (b);
CRDP, Caen: p. 65 (m);
DITE: pp. 23(b), 34-35, 43 (h);
CRHQ/Université de Caen/M.Desgardin/J.Quellien: pp. 18, 36-37, 62-63, 69, 82, 102, 122;
DR: p. 51 (b), 105 (t);
Éditions Normandes Legoubey: pp. 2 (c, d, f, g), 19 (b), 25 (bd), 32-33, 45, 46 (m), 48 (t), 50-51, 66 (m), 71 (m), 72 (h), 76 (h), 78-79, 90 (br), 92, 108 (t), 120;
Éditions Normandes Legoubey/Batterie de Merville collection: p. 127;
Imperial War Museum, London: pp. 8, 10, 11 (tr), 24 (b), 59 (b), 61 (b), 65 (b), 66 (t), 68 (b & m), 74 (tl), 76 (br), 89 (t), 94 (t), 95 (t), 104 (t), 108 (b), 109 (b), 115 (b), 116, 117 (t & bl), 118 (t), 119 (m);
Imperial War Museum, London/America-Gold collection: p. 61 (t);
Imperial War Museum, London/J.P.Benamou collection: p. 70 (b), 98, 124 (t), 126 (t);
Musée America-Gold: p. 77 (t);
Musée de la Liberté: p. 31 (ml);
Musée Général de Gaulle: p. 77 (b);
Musée D-Day Omaha: p. 49 (tr);
Musée du Débarquement: p. 31 (bl);
Musée Mémorial Bataille de Normandie/J.P.Benamou: p. 75 (b);
Musée des Rangers: p. 49 (br);
National Archives USA: pp. 3 (b), 11 (tl), 23 (t), 27 (m), 28 (m), 30 (t), 33 (b), 39 (t), 48 (b), 53 (b & r), 56 (t), 57 (tl), 67 (tl);
National Archives USA/B.Paich: p. 47;
National Archives USA/J.P.Benamou collection: pp. 17, 20 (t);
National Archives Canada: pp. 9 (b), 79 (b), 80, 81 (t), 85 (b), 86 (t), 87 (t), 107, 112 (b);
ONAC 14: pp. 2 (a), 3 (bd), 38 (m), 39 (b), 40 (t & b), 41, 42 (b), 43 (b), 48 (tr), 49 (tr, m & bl), 52 (b), 53 (t & m), 54 (b & tl), 55, 56 (m), 57 (b), 65 (tr), 66 (b), 67 (b), 73 (t), 75 (tm, ml, & bm), 76 (bl), 77 (m), 84 (tl), 85 (tr), 95 (b), 100 (t), 110 (tm, bl & br), 111 (b & tr), 121 (br);
Patricia Canino: p. 113 (b).

Conception and Design

Nathalie Moraud
4, rue de l'Éguillon - 14970 Bénouville

Printer : KAPP, Evreux
Legal registration : July 2004